scars on th seehors

bill bissett

talonbooks 1999

Published with the assistance of the Canada Council for the Arts.

We acknowledge the financial support of the Government of Canada through the Book Publishing Industry Development Program for our publishing activities.   Canadä

Talonbooks
#104—3100 Production Way
Burnaby, British Columbia, Canada V5A 4R4

Typeset in Librarian and printed and bound in Canada by Hignell Printing Ltd.
First Printing: April 1999

Talonbooks are distributed in Canada by General Distribution Services, 325 Humber College Blvd., Toronto, Ontario, Canada M9W 7C3; Tel.:(416) 213-1919; Fax:(416) 213-1917.
Talonbooks are distributed in the U.S.A. by General Distribution Services Inc.,85 Rock River Drive, Suite 202, Buffalo, New York, U.S.A. 14207-2170; Tel.:1-800-805-1083; Fax:1-800-481-6207.

sum uv thees pomes previouslee apeerd in *bomb thret* miniapolis *descant* toronto *qween street quartrlee* toronto *poesia totale* mantua *capilano review* north vancouvr *fiddlebead* frederikton n on th 1999 audio cassett *off th road   a bluebird* seattle

a trip 2 th moon was performd at pacifik cinematek   vancouvr jan 98 commisyund by th vancouvr writrs festival

Canadian Cataloguing in Publication Data

Bissett, Bill, 1939-
Scars on the seehors

Poems.
ISBN 0-88922-387-4

I. Title.
PS8503.I78S32 1999   C811'.54   C99-910224-9
PR9199.3.B45S32 1999

thanks 2 th ontario arts council writrs reserv 1998 via
descant magazeen   th vancouvr writrs festival   in2
print magazeen capilano review talonbooks patrick
friesen n sharon thiesen n th fort nashwak motel
frederikton new brunswick

speshul thanks as well 2 UNB english dept frederikton

n 2 sandie drzewiecki   much thanks

watching   broadcast nus

i see th salmon talks will
                    resume on monday

well thank god at leest th
                    salmon ar talking

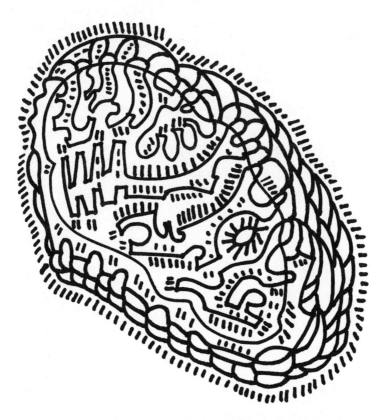

sequences uv ekstasee

th wintr peopul

ar responding 2 th green hous effekt evree
few yeers they find it 2 warm n go furthr

north 4 comfort toronto is now 2 cozee 4
them th sault n thundr bay r far 2 summree

they feel th warmth 2 b frivolous it makes
them un eezee   7 yeers ago aftr having found

nu liskeard 2 mediterranean th wintr peopul
discovr church hill falls 2 b mor balmee thn

they wud want n ar hedding tord th artik
circul evn ther they bcame restless   th artik

was warming up   if it heets up   evree wher
wher will th wintr peopul go   full uv needs 4

snow n icikul pellets flying in th freezing rain
n snow hills n mountains mooving around th

elk n polar bears   th sun glayzing on th ice
fields   th hallusinating cold n steem from

theyr wishes 4 th souls fire not distraktid by
anee gud wethr

INSIDE TH BRAIN

                              perry was telling michael
george n me

                    th doktors wer certinlee consernd abt
      th eighteen month old baybee   th x rays showd a
      tumor   inside his brain   n it was
                                     growing

   sew they operatid pulld out th huge doubul kiwi sizd
                tumor   th baybee was fine n is still
                        thriving with no reoccurens
               uv anee tumors

   th tumor howevr is still growing is not malignant
  nd its living cells r duplikating themselvs now they
          need a whol building 2 hous it whn
                  inishulee they needid onlee
       a small part uv wun lab

             now th doubul kiwi needs manee labs
  a labyrinth uv rooms   soon a whol complex uv
    buildings living cells multiply   thees dew not
         stop GROWING   its a growing cells
  4get abt yr METAPHORS   ths may meen we can heel
      burnt bodeez sew manee condishyuns   asking
       4 regrowth eye sd
                      anothr building is
    filling up with living cells we cant breeth
  we have no space   we hope 2 jettison back 2 zaktra
  its now uninhabitid altho rumors uv th reesons 4 its
             empteeness   can b disquieting evn
      disturbing

                  BINNNNNG michael sd   wev
              got 2 get   GOOINNNG

its like unrequitid love isint it jimmee sd

yu survive it by leeving town at leest in yr mind
yu xcise a part uv yrselvs n live with less uv yr
self that phase that yu fall 4 sum wun whos no
gud 4 yu it turns out cant fullee or matchinglee
return yr bodee 4 them is oftn sumwher els or
adrift leeving yu touring th nu place a citizen
uv love can it catch up with yu proaktivlee un
puzzul yu pull th errant parts uv yr psyches
selvs in from howevr afar yu fell dumb in th
tall kastul peopul talk uv a full moon cumming
soon yu preserv yr life opn it up 4 dessert on a
cold wintrs nite from th basement up th creekee
steps th jar sparkling peeches strawbereez in th
snow tasteing th solving mixtyurs with th ice
kreem gradualee footstep by hand held ther is
no them we lite canduls on th mirakul taybul n
yu dont know th reesons or motivs 4 being wher
its all caut up in eye wake up say je suis
citoyen d'amour we ar in a state uv bliss our
third eyez opn n sharing we ar inkandescent eye
remembr love we did evreething 4 each othr evree
day evree nite full our hearts wud rise 2 get it on
n ride our dreem horses in 2 th sky we moov th
danse changing nu partnrs we dew evreething 4 n
with each othr burn up our time we dont know
its time caut by surprize in th dansing its an
othr storee anothr love we bgin 2 live with ourselvs
n our journeez n our changing beleefs whn eye
cum 2 meet its not 2 leen on its 2 share eye
wake up lounge inside th clouds blanket moovd
aside say i am a citizen uv love we felt our danse
eye dont know who its 4 aneemor we bcum incan
descent cum heer eye feel our bones n flesh stir
yu call 4 me th wires n telepathee ball th air

my fathr in his bed room th morning i left

in a weird way i was starting 2 like him he was
loosning up a bit thru th greef uv my first mothr
going 2 spirit n his feeling less pressurd now by
doktors n operaysyuns n was th worst ovr yet

maybe he was starting 2 like me   my boy frend who
i was in love with wud stay ovr upstares with me in
th green attik   fathr wud b nice 2 us both i still wud
take his cookeez n milk 2 him b4 he was going 2 bed

at nite as always sins my mothr went 2 spirit n he
wud say up th stairs gud nite 2 us both he wud still
skreem at my oldr sistrs me yelling at him 4 them tho
he left his estate 2 them i dont know what it was nowun

evr told me he was yelling at them less tho it was all
mor thn i cud undrstand always had bin tho i tried
2 sumtimes blamed him 4 most uv it othrwize iud
blamd myself wch i reelee oftn did internalizing th
pressurs n whn wud he start skreeming n blaming
us agen th erupsyuns wer unpredicktabul n uncawsd

like th patreearkal god but ther was a parshul tendrness
beginning   n i was leeving me n my boy frend getting
out   we had reseevd 2 manee cawsyunaree messages
subliminal n overt tales uv what it wud b like if we wer
2 stay ther in halifax 2 soldyeer on with our love ther

told fathr i had a job with his frend who ran general
motors in calgary it was erlee morning no warning he
was getting up now in his pajamas i sd we wantid an
erlee start on th road whn th rides wud b best

he sd gudbye son   i think he knew ther reelee was no
such job at general motors in calgary with his frend

me n my boy frend wer going 2 leev western civilizaysyun
n b happee 4evr how diffrent was th rest uv th world

all th rivrs uv our lives

th hunee uv our dayze th murmurs uv
th treez in th icikul breez

his hous was bside th rivr
n altho in wintr it did freez
th beautee uv th place was sew mooving
th lite pink n orange lite streeming
thru th treez with th goldn hues n
brown n red uv th bark n th continuous
white n blu n oranges uv snow
sew tall evreewher

he wud turn th logs ovr in th grate keep th
fire going n wundr wud he settul heer or a
fireplace in th citee wher
othrs like him he cud hang with oftn he
xperiensd veree narrow escapes from th
judgmental diskovereez th linear anee
wing dicksyunareez n heer hunee thers no
wun els tho what can that meen   working

around a nite   evreething duz not need 2 b
thredid thru a yunifying whole

wud sum wun   sum day
rise from th rivr 2 sleep with him
4evr wanting him

11

i was in th whirlwind

i was in th whirlwind
   place uv ego demands

i was in th whirlwind
   o all th flying biting sand

i was in th fieree furnace
   place uv hot konflikts

i was in th fieree furnace
   wher sum peopul get
      theyr licks

but i wantid 2 go up on th
  northern medow wher ium
now   letting go   letting go
     letting go   letting go

o if ther wer a love 4 me
  2 sleep with 4 a whil

watching wintr cum in seeing
  wintr fall   2 sleep with 4
 a whil   undr th cumming snow
        undr th cumming snow
         undr th cumming snow
          undr th cummin snow

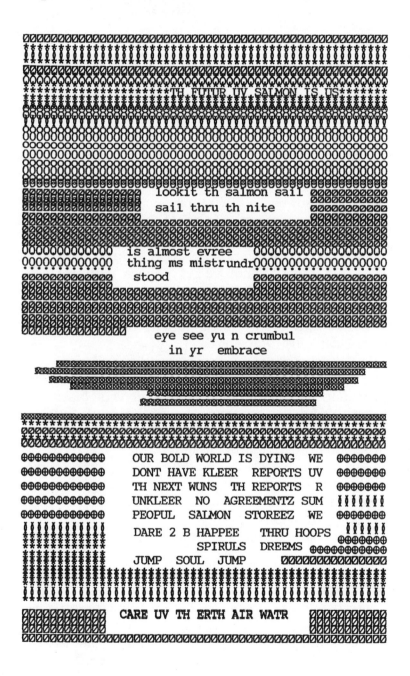

TH FUTUR UV SALMON IS US

lookit th salmon sail
sail thru th nite

is almost evree
thing ms mistrundr
stood

eye see yu n crumbul
in yr embrace

OUR BOLD WORLD IS DYING   WE
DONT HAVE KLEER   REPORTS UV
TH NEXT WUNS TH REPORTS R
UNKLEER   NO   AGREEMENTZ SUM
PEOPUL   SALMON   STOREEZ   WE
DARE 2 B HAPPEE   THRU HOOPS
              SPIRULS   DREEMS
JUMP   SOUL   JUMP

CARE UV TH ERTH AIR WATR

inkompleet mewsings   on such a slendr
threding

we ar heer th long maroond ovr th irrigatid waver
       ing sand rock newlee emerging watr
   taybuls   mavis ovr th delta rivard on th see
       wall our hearts dew yu evr feel
   how th marroon changes ther ar diffrent
       marvara text aisles marvara bliss
destinee   charaktr sir madam cumstances intr
seksyuns coinsidens eyez uv wch bee holdrs
fevrs   take it eezee turn it on evr sew softlee
it is sd how nowun gets what they want we lern
2 love what we ar getting   all things being equal
we find it interesting wherevr we ar n lern
     ing 2 want what we get   thees ar th rocks
in yr hed ium returning   th masheeneree uv
     grudging without wch 2 hold on 2 sum
minusha uv event   meeningless on its owning
what   air fire watr erth

beautiful hart crane had a familee home in key west
lardr pantreez wrapping porches he was fascinatid
   with th familee life ther   powrful peopul in th
     familee   in nu york citee 18 or 20 moovd 2
apartment ovrlooking brooklyn bridg lasere th
   architect uv th bridg had livd in th same room
all three crane garcia lorca n lasere livd in th
same apartment at diffrent timez nevr met   a
wayze from kalamazoo
     hart n me running from offishuls

     taste th mangos see th mongees tapestreed
meditaysyuns wafting fall from th wishing juniper
   zeebra treez   dripping dreems uv cumming in
my mouth my bodee turning in 2 yu   fluiditee yr
bodee cumming in 2 my evr opning mouths uv
       ecstasee being

it was a dreem they sd reassuringlee loosing th
finessing tides n th heeling

uv suddnlee beauteez uv touch n kissing evree
wher all th opnings fulfilling branches linen all
sew oxygen saliva silkee tongue animal lick suck
n plunge in2 each othr sew whn they re enterd th
room th heet n humiditee 2 kleen up aftr 2 re let
ther was no wun ther   in that 4 us   sumptuous
place

we had gone on   not thru th doors or windows
they did xamine theyr brows raisd xtendid 2 th
qwestyun perhaps we had nevr reelee chekd in
ther

marvaarraa   bliss

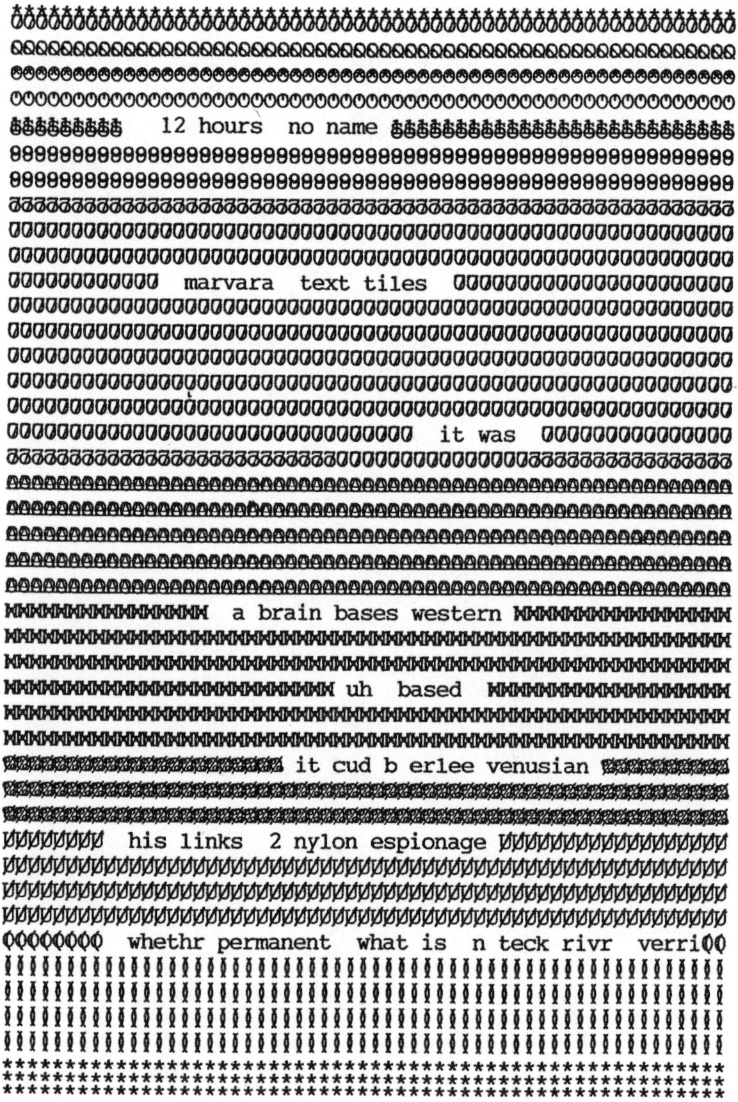

ÕÕ
ΩΩΩΩΩΩΩΩΩΩΩΩΩΩΩΩΩΩΩΩΩΩΩΩΩΩΩΩΩΩΩΩΩΩΩΩΩΩΩΩΩΩΩΩΩΩΩΩΩΩΩΩΩΩΩΩΩΩΩΩΩΩΩΩΩΩΩ
ᎧᎧᎧ
OOOOOOOOOOOOOOOOOOOOOOOOOOOOOOOOOOOOOOOOOOOOOOOOOOOOOOOOOOOOOO
ᕫᕫᕫᕫᕫᕫᕫᕫ   12 hours   no name ᕫᕫᕫᕫᕫᕫᕫᕫᕫᕫᕫᕫᕫᕫᕫᕫᕫᕫᕫᕫᕫᕫᕫᕫ
ᑫᑫᑫ
ᑫᑫᑫ
ᘔᘔᘔ
ᘮᘮᘮ
ᘮᘮᘮ
ᘮᘮᘮᘮᘮᘮᘮᘮᘮᘮᘮᘮ marvara text tiles ᘮᘮᘮᘮᘮᘮᘮᘮᘮᘮᘮᘮᘮᘮᘮᘮᘮᘮ
ᘮᘮ
ᘮᘮ
ᘮᘮ
ᘮᘮ
ᘮᘮ
ᘮᘮᘮᘮᘮᘮᘮᘮᘮᘮᘮᘮᘮᘮᘮᘮᘮᘮᘮᘮᘮᘮᘮᘮ it was ᘮᘮᘮᘮᘮᘮᘮᘮᘮᘮᘮᘮ
ᘔᘔᘔᘔᘔᘔᘔᘔᘔᘔᘔᘔᘔᘔᘔᘔᘔᘔᘔᘔᘔᘔᘔᘔᘔᘮᘮᘮᘮᘮᘮᘮᘮᘮᘮᘮᘮᘔᘔᘔᘔᘔᘔᘔᘔᘔᘔᘔᘔᘔᘔᘔ
ᗺᗺ
ᗺᗺ
ᗺᗺ
ᗺᗺ
ᗺᗺ
ᙢᙢᙢᙢᙢᙢᙢᙢᙢᙢᙢᙢᙢᙢ a brain bases western ᙢᙢᙢᙢᙢᙢᙢᙢᙢᙢᙢᙢᙢᙢ
ᙢᙢᙢ
ᙢᙢᙢ
ᙢᙢᙢᙢᙢᙢᙢᙢᙢᙢᙢᙢᙢᙢᙢᙢᙢᙢᙢ uh   based   ᙢᙢᙢᙢᙢᙢᙢᙢᙢᙢᙢᙢᙢᙢᙢ
ᙢᙢᙢ
ᙢᙢᙢ
▩▩▩▩▩▩▩▩▩▩▩▩▩ it cud b erlee venusian ▩▩▩▩▩▩▩▩
▩▩
▩▩
ᘃᘃᘃᘃᘃᘃᘃᘃ his links 2 nylon espionage ᘃᘃᘃᘃᘃᘃᘃᘃᘃᘃᘃᘃ
ᘃᘃᘃ
ᘃᘃᘃ
ᘃᘃᘃ
OOOOOOOO whethr permanent what is n teck rivr verriOO
ƗƗ
ƗƗ
ƗƗ
ƗƗ
****
****
****

troubul in trestul town

my hed is made uv cabbage
my hed is made uv cabbage
my hed is made uv cabbage
my hed is made uv cabbage

my cabbage is made uv
infinit heds ar they shining
with peoneez   mortal
fires

inside them numbrless memoreez from b4
emptee places 2 fill up with nows bcumming endless b4s n
gaps or neurologia holding cells gasping gapeing 4 what aftr i
dont sumtimes have anee knowing uv how what they it hmmm
represent sd desire 2 moov dreem crawl along side th rail way
tracks pell mell answring veto tantalizing plodjunning give me sum
sugar is that it   **my eyez ar** duke maranger yelpd his mouth th
mosyun uv agonizing skreems a perfekt oval uv woes

falling out pleez paste them back in along th alabastr hotel
sliding down from th top uv th riff all th ghosts they changd theyr
minds aftr smiling memoreez uv a stranger nite at th coppr mine
bargoes th entreez b4 ths they wer going 2 my hed is made uv
such cabbage sumtimes evreething sinks in close up dishes
fall in th sink no reeson just th vibraysyun uv ystrday n th daring
disastrs ium undr th rail way tracks xploding with sugar my
buttons eyez pop out what is it sereen travl thru th space n th
place places post cards cumming 2 us   ther they ar
on top uv a purpul elephant his eyez goldn loving
geographika analogia   eye rest from ths
uranium planet   maroon   cabbage green th
palest green like a slivr   uv moonlite undr th
hovel stares we found   sucking th frenzeed eye
slit th lettis leeving by th   side door   tippee toeing
they ar aftr all   balling on th porch swing not
needing th xtra kompanee have 2 go work ork kor w krr
w owwwwwwwww wo wo yr oats n th stranguling cabbage
cribbage uv wango wher w w 2 4 grimps th wind
closd th subway doors was th lettrs uv shredding n masturd
wuh wuh sumtimes its cauliflowr densiteez or abjekt prayrs
we beleev finalee in th invisibul th visibul is 2 unreliant a dash
thundrbird up 2 beleef agen nevr falling b4 th realism sword
a playr five herons bracing 4 th flite an undulant swan sensing
sumthing els we still dont know with malt salt falt on them evn n
thats how mistr fens driveway n frozn broadloooommmmmm

uv kours i cant know how its shiftid until its dun
n is it evr dun   or

MOR FUR THN FUREE

fortitude ovr western weer

isolatid from theyr own grudge
masheeneree th insident itself
was without am or

anee meening

th
l
e
s
s
ons uv xxx

living with less on

ther is sumwun outside uv th soshul konstrukts

nowun has th rite 2 tell yu what 2 dew no mattr
  what they think   yu ar 2 them AND no way
yu can make sumwun reelee love yu aneemor whn
theyv got enuff out uv yu   OR   they moovd on
        fine sew yu   get lonlee sumtimez   th habit uv
dragging sum wun in 2 yr spideree well   laying guilt
or attachment trips on them 4get it telepathiko i sd 2
him let that   go   get on with   yr own life   that
trewlee xists can b sew radiant wundrful regardless
uv th tapes whos with yu yr involvments in th big
soshul meening ful konstrukts lift

eye in	eye out	eet in	we cant know
dreem inn	dreeming	inning	soups on
soupcon	50-100 specees	bcum	xtinkt
evree day	th mooving	show	dna writes is
intaglio	moovs on	will it all	b plasteek til
th last layrs	no longr possibul	2 pull	aneething
mor back	pleez dont nag me	pleez dont	nattr
me	yu have no rite	all we can dew	is love

ther is no ideel evreewun if anee wun fails from in thees
dimensyuns   obligato   fell snore sum mixing in supp
lianto   nevrths or that rain   ploundring in 2 wat
sing thn anothr call came thru self ironeez piling up hill
start   agen   n ferris sonata lyrik sum   ironing
sonnett   reel   epik prsonae narrateef cineam veritay
dramateek mono log whn we can track our selvs eesilee
enuff 2 give up self destruktiv environ mentalee destruktiv
love sex powr games testing 2 much try trust love being
            evree day 50-100 specees bcum xtinkt
     evree day 50-100 specees bcum xtinkt
dew peopul think peopul will b th last 2 go take out
   or have inn we thot we cudint stop th brutalitee
we thot we cud work on th texts n ourselvs inside
out side ther is no diffrens ium not th same as th
group kokooning 2 vast illusyuns being alriteness n
go 2 th deus exsetera *pleez feed th peopul who we all
ar zophtara pleedid with them in song*

itself
th words dew

```
        themselvs  gathr     in2
    a strengthening     or
          letting       go
uv        each        ordring
    n        tripping       th
feathrs         n          ankuls
    changing    love        n
    feeling     uv        onlee
        2        b        2gethr
       how     it can       b
     again      yes        what
      can        u         ask
        4        or         try
     xcept      what        is
    alredee     givn       that
      we        find       sum
    living      space       n
      air       breeth     in2
      yu        heart      veins
        2       moov       tord
   what          yu        bcum
    equal       with        n
    what         yu         on
      yr        knees        2
      can         eet       uv
       n         what       th
     prson       can       eet
   uv yu         entr      yu    take
    n give      from       yu
       is         n        that
        2        is       onlee
      part        uv        th
                thred
               threding
                 yu
```

```
████████████████████████████████████████████
████████████████████████████████████████████
████████████████████████████████████████████
████████████████████████████████████████████
                    OPEN    HEER
████████████████████████████████████████████
████████████████████████████████████████████
████████████████████████████████████████████
████████████████████████████████████████████
```

██████████████████████████████ ████████ PEEL
███████████████████████████   BACK 2 OPEN ███
ᴜᴜ
ᴜᴜ
ᵠᵠᵠᵠᵠᵠᵠᵠᵠᵠᵠᵠᵠ ths is how it starts 2
ᵠᵠᵠᵠᵠᵠᵠᵠᵠᵠᵠᵠᵠᵠᵠᵠᵠᵠᵠᵠᵠᵠᵠᵠᵠᵠ happn th
ᵠᵠᵠᵠᵠᵠᵠᵠᵠᵠ disks start separating from
th rest uv th bodee th disks upstare in th
    attik   uv th quote mind n swirling away on
theyr own unrelatid 2 bodilee activiteez or
    barelee th phone rings agensee n in answring
its a farming metaphor separating n th milk uv
    zeeon captures th shining sapphires they werent
    reel amethysts still lovlee tho n what all
didint we say xchange THEES AR TH DISKS WITH
    TH TAPES IN THEM farming thots letting them
all go pass thru a thot form is a thot farm is
    a thot form is a thot form is a thot farming
sumtimes yu cud cry all day n nite ovr th fals
    accusing n th brokn promises if ths is a way
t bcum mstrustful mistr uv othrs ther is no othr
yu cudint have pickd a bettr way our lives on hold
bcoz uv th othrs admonishyuns propa ganda eye
    want 2 skreem █████████████████████████████
ᴜᴜᴜᴜᴜᴜᴜᴜᴜᴜᴜᴜᴜᴜᴜᴜᴜᴜᴜᴜᴜᴜᴜᴜᴜᴜᴜᴜᴜᴜ turning down th
    tifanee lamp he nustuld in closr 2 him th tapes
let go now n they cud get in 2 a beautiful 69
    n love each othr hunee bfor its 2 late thats
    all we can dew th leedrs ar fuckd th advice
givrs alredee destroyd th etsetera remembr
whn all we wantid was jam n peenut buttr sand
    wch is n hugging n storeez n NO STOREEZ
    N EACH OTHR ███████████████████████████
███
                ███████████████████████
                ·······················

21

```
爨爨爨爨爨爨爨爨爨爨爨爨爨爨爨爨爨爨爨爨爨爨爨爨爨爨爨爨爨爨爨爨爨爨爨爨爨爨爨爨爨爨爨爨
```
th dance uv th toxeek neurona voices in th
```
ΦΦΦΦΦΦΦΦΦΦΦΦΦΦΦΦΦΦΦΦΦΦΦΦ laundraoon ΦΦΦΦΦΦΦΦΦΦΦΦΦΦΦΦΦΦΦΦΦΦΦΦ
}}}}}}}}}}}}}}}}}}}}}}}}}}}}}}}}}}}}}}}}}}}}}}}}}}}}}}}}}}}}}}}
***********************************************************
```
laundroon sew immersd in life dew we have free
will dterminism choices b inside evreewun sum
times not floundring isolatid dances occur b in
side th mewsik soshulizing fine not always need
id rock in th bars th rhythm changes illusyuns
uv free will whn we think we have a chois whn in
fakt we chood what is alredee writtn 4 us th sew
unkritikul crush uv love we thrill 2 changes us
angeleek sd th importans uv langwages not speek
ing words ar bridges take us 2 othr spheers whn
th words start in th dansing go as longs i can
without them in2 th mewsik thn i look 4 th navi
gator ache powr in a curv a longing in th heet
rivr its possibul 2 b happee evn tho a prson we
love is not happee or is its us what if ths is
th onlee life with ths ego supr id prsona etsetera
th is is prettee n supr he undrlines yes yes eye
sd fr sure we cant relees evreething like its a
totalitarian sylogism return 2 merlin chopra get
on bord th tentakuls ar cumming th voices in th
laundroon ar materializine maintenent n ar shaping th air
```
ᵇmᵐᵐᵐᵐᵐᵐᵐᵐᵐᵐᵐᵐᵐᵐᵐᵐᵐᵐᵐᵐᵐᵐᵐᵐᵐᵐᵐᵐᵐᵐᵐᵐᵐᵐᵐᵐᵐᵐᵐᵐᵐᵐᵐᵐᵐᵐᵐᵐᵐᵐᵐ
δδδδδδδδδδδδδδδδδδδδδδδδδδδδδδδδδδδδδδδδδδδδδδδδδδδδδδδδδδδδδδδ⁶
θθθθθθθθθθθθθθθθθθθθθθθθθθθθθθθθθθθθθθθθθθθθθθθθθθθθθθθθθθθθθθθ*
θθθθθθθθθθθθθθθθθθθθθθθθθθθθθθθθθθθθθθθθθθθθθθθθθθθθθθθθθθθθθθθ*
‡‡‡‡‡‡‡‡‡‡‡‡‡‡‡‡‡‡‡‡‡‡‡‡‡‡‡‡‡‡‡‡‡‡‡‡‡‡‡‡‡‡‡‡‡‡‡‡‡‡‡‡‡‡‡‡‡‡‡*
‡‡‡‡‡‡‡‡‡‡‡‡‡‡‡‡‡‡‡‡‡‡‡‡‡‡‡‡‡‡‡‡‡‡‡‡‡‡‡‡‡‡‡‡‡‡‡‡‡‡‡‡‡‡‡‡‡‡‡‡‡*
‡‡‡‡‡‡‡‡‡‡‡‡‡‡‡‡‡‡‡‡‡‡‡‡‡‡‡‡‡‡‡‡‡‡‡‡‡‡‡‡‡‡‡‡‡‡‡‡‡‡‡‡‡‡‡‡‡‡‡‡‡*
‡‡‡‡‡‡‡‡‡‡‡‡‡‡‡‡‡‡‡‡‡‡‡‡‡‡‡‡‡‡‡‡‡‡‡‡‡‡‡‡‡‡‡‡‡‡‡‡‡‡‡‡‡‡‡‡‡‡‡‡‡‡
ΩΩΩΩΩΩΩΩΩΩΩΩΩΩΩΩΩΩΩΩΩΩΩΩΩΩΩΩΩΩΩΩΩΩΩΩΩΩΩΩΩΩΩΩΩΩΩΩΩΩΩΩΩΩΩΩΩΩΩΩ
℧℧℧℧℧℧℧℧℧℧℧℧℧℧℧℧℧℧℧℧℧℧℧℧℧℧℧℧℧℧℧℧℧℧℧℧℧℧℧℧℧℧℧℧℧℧℧℧℧℧℧℧℧℧℧℧℧℧℧℧
ᴟᴟᴟᴟᴟᴟᴟᴟᴟᴟᴟᴟᴟᴟᴟᴟᴟᴟᴟᴟᴟᴟᴟᴟᴟᴟᴟᴟᴟᴟᴟᴟᴟᴟᴟᴟᴟᴟᴟᴟᴟᴟᴟᴟᴟᴟᴟᴟᴟᴟᴟᴟᴟᴟᴟ
▨▨▨▨▨▨▨▨▨▨▨▨▨▨▨▨▨▨▨▨▨▨▨▨▨▨▨▨▨▨▨▨▨▨▨▨▨▨▨▨▨▨▨▨▨▨▨▨▨▨▨▨▨▨▨▨▨▨▨
▨▨▨▨▨▨▨▨▨▨▨▨▨▨▨▨▨▨▨▨▨▨▨▨▨▨▨▨▨▨▨▨▨▨▨▨▨▨▨▨▨▨▨▨▨▨▨▨▨▨▨▨▨▨▨▨▨▨▨▨
ⱮⱮⱮⱮⱮⱮⱮⱮⱮⱮⱮⱮⱮⱮⱮⱮⱮⱮⱮⱮⱮⱮⱮⱮⱮⱮⱮⱮⱮⱮⱮⱮⱮⱮⱮⱮⱮⱮⱮⱮⱮⱮⱮⱮⱮⱮⱮⱮⱮⱮⱮⱮⱮⱮⱮ
▨▨▨▨▨▨▨▨▨▨▨▨▨▨▨▨▨▨▨▨▨▨▨▨▨▨▨▨▨▨▨▨▨▨▨▨▨▨▨▨▨▨▨▨▨▨▨▨▨▨▨▨▨▨▨▨▨▨▨▨
▨▨▨▨▨▨▨▨▨▨▨▨▨▨▨▨▨▨▨▨▨▨▨▨▨▨▨▨▨▨▨▨▨▨▨▨▨▨▨▨▨▨▨▨▨▨▨▨▨▨▨▨▨▨▨▨▨▨▨▨
▨▨▨▨▨▨▨▨▨▨▨▨▨▨▨▨▨▨▨▨▨▨▨▨▨▨▨▨▨▨▨▨▨▨▨▨▨▨▨▨▨▨▨▨▨▨▨▨▨▨▨▨▨▨▨▨▨▨▨▨
each  window  n eye lay bside th lowest mildewd crane
thinking uv th unending smile in each wave as if it is th
hevn moment we cud continualee prseev  what  thees shirts
whats bothring  them  2 much  rain  maybe itul change soon
canoe  its so nowher 2 figur  mine th bodee  mind n bodee
```
ΦΦΦΦΦΦΦΦΦΦΦΦΦΦΦΦΦΦΦΦΦΦΦΦΦΦΦΦΦΦΦΦΦΦΦΦΦΦΦΦΦΦΦΦΦΦΦΦ
‡‡‡‡‡‡‡‡‡‡‡‡‡‡‡‡‡‡‡‡‡‡‡‡‡‡ᴟᴟᴟᴟᴟᴟᴟᴟᴟᴟᴟᴟᴟᴟᴟᴟᴟᴟᴟᴟᴟ
```
```

it usd 2 b

4 konrad white n ken thomsod

yu cud get sum toilet papr
nd a newspapr both 4
a dollr fiftee

now yu cant   yu gotta
make a chois

mistr n ms wintr

th wher uv kours can b veree much part uv th is   out uv
auto neurologia thot forms thot farming   ther ar
eyez in back uv our heds yes write what is ar
watr ovr our bodeez th karibu nite stars
erth breething loving whats calld naytyur th
blessings alredee givn restorativ feed th fire brown
rice with raisins steemd   vegeez camomile t tor
onto no canadian ideels uv wun type font onlee
much mor brik is grown heer in centralia
thn in th western coastal area in
vancouvr psychik restif pacifika energizing
spirits home same as heer diffrent heer winds
gusting ovr toronto   nausea uv prolonging staying
in doors snow falling on crisp 17 below b4 th
wind chill faktora   on turtul island   mistr n ms
wintr mooving ovr ths vast geographee
in sew manee langwages nowun can feel in
dominant mode   mistr n ms wintr ar saying th
cornr we think we ar finding ourselvs in is curving
working not onlee th tops uv our heds delite in
being   feel th chill from th sun room put th
heetr in cozee carree a candul in sit around
levitate laff languish lounge love lavish lick
laff agen   mistr n ms wintr puttin such a huge

blanket ovr us all th tangereen whisprs n
cloudee snow crystals blush th tides n fog th
hail cant see a thing th air is sew filld with
swirling beings inside we see evreething   out
side th snow monstrs walk n trod th erth
n th 1950s moscow architecktyur th post modern
elegans th hurried gentrified n th brik bedrooms
sew tiny against theyr brushing snow thighs 20
storeez tall th childrn onlee uv mistr n ms
wintr puttin on theyr snow coats rocks th

24

neighbourhood we ar sew small inside seriouslee
         konsidr our mortalitee our eyez widen
with each othr as th glass wavers n shakes as
                    mistr n ms wintr walk down th
         frozn street   with theyr familee our
                    streets crack what
         can we dew put anothr pot uv t on
n reed from veree old texts abt th seeming
         changing uv ordinaree or customaree
vishyuns 2 th xtraordinaree n revelatoree
         hallusinaysyuns uv what alredee was is
did sumthing happn th ball we live on sew manee
thanks 2 gravitee we stay on   smallr thn its
         hairs us suspending in space we make a
biggr nois 2 ourselvs thn aneething we ar
         wud warrant th food hunt etsetera othr
creeshurs thees snow spirit beings   much
         mor monumental phenomenal thn ourselvs
strangr thn ficksyun walk among us we have
         no words 4   whn things ar ordinaree we can
         dismiss   whn th buildings moov we dare 2
         stare out th windows   watch th candul keep
breething   mistr n ms wintr will pass thru weul

         heer abt them   in sum othr countreez cawsing
         floods   ava lanches   they dont meen 2 they
              wud love us if they cud see us   they ar sew
                    tall we cant see theyr heds   n we look
                         out n marvel

mistr n ms wintr answr 2 second part uv qwestyun
7 in intrview by **adeena karasick** *how duz yr environ
ment affekt yr writing karibu coastal centralia* mor
from ths intrview in next book **b leevabul charaktrs**

yes

i think i cud live full time with sum wun
but i dont know if its rite 4 me on ths
planet   or

i dont know if ths is th rite planet 4 me
2 dew that yet arint ther othr planets

uv kours zaktra from wher
me n sum uv my frends
cum now visiting heer with
me on erth n thees strange
erthling wayze   sigh

suspendid balls in space erth sun moon
agenseez quaint n dreemee sumtimez
what was b4 whats cumming reelee
they fight n kill abt theyr versyuns
n take plutonium in2 space n feed
chickn shit 2 cows kill peopul with
lethal pharmasuitakuls

a place 4 trew love they assur
us now thats fr sure within out
side th margins uv th battuls
uv th rich on2 th poor n trying
2 get out uv th lines uv fire yet
working 4 principals n our belleez
n taste buds n chill at leest 4

an eternal seeming second or first n
grateful 4 th mewsik sumtimez in our
heds cums from nowher we can name
nowun is defined by th group theyr
allegidlee in tho we may need 2 feel
that consciousness oftn n regardless
letting go uv th dedlee othr games

th kaptin sd he was mercurial

eye sd i usd 2 be

tho n mercuree yes

that band is veree strong aftr

now i mostlee live in th words n images

mirage n orages n self eves pleezes

thats oranges

remembr thos dayze n nites in marvara

ah marvara he sighd

th long marin
on th irrigatid mesa
mirrors th delta
is in dangr th

ridge maroon
in our hearts
dew yu evr get
th feel uv

m a r v a a r a

th souls fieree in marvara

                    not onlee th empire
              dare 2 b happee 4 ourselvs

  th dolphin peopul sew barelee lapping bravelee
thru th junk n gloree dioxins poisons n fresh oxygen
burning sum timez what we fastn on   is th leest
likelee possibilitee

    we had side skirtid th lizard life sew insayshabul
dwelling huts sparkling
                  not 2 worree abt th 4tress in th soul
        sumtimes eye need sex 4 self esteem   or 4 life

is ths what it is or a part uv it   whns he gonna call

    ths is 2day not ystrday   not 2morrow

  all th dayze uv no sun shine gradualee illumine
sew th disapeering objekts heer   th teems uv cats
theyr gold eyez   invade th lizards   dwellings
                              atoms shreeking
                              ther is no absolute
                              lafftr gess n dance
                              wheet fields gerania
                              ium sew gladiola 2
                                meet yu thees
                                    treez o
        4 a thousand yeers holding n
      lavishing th rain 2 th red mud kleering th
      souls fieree   th soul is fire   welcum 2 our
        world   what dew yu think   its how we ar
    ar yu looking at th marvara   marvara text iles

28

marvaar tex stiles iles th futur uv salmon is us
                                        isint it
    thos nites in marvara   ahhhhhh
        if th salmon go sew will we   ar yu looking 4
    th beginning uv time   yr selvs love is alredee
        inside yu whn we met it was in marvara our
lives wer maroon d intangentshul reveeling our we
    bcum ourselvs   ther wer sevn islands around
    marvara   sevn central pleysyurs eeting making
love bathing hiking resting laffing sleeping being
2gethr boats btween wud delivr us aftr a full day
uv working 2 find agen ourselvs moov out uv th
    huge treez   dew yu have th receipe   can yu reed
th direksyuns   a whirlwind roman isint it 2 share
    can we   n b yrself sum mite call foolish   allo
        allo   its yr call yr selvs th tides changing brek
th streem   we walkd ovr land 4 kilometrs rainbows n
majeek lightning   th pickshurs in th lettrs sum
    langwages   kultur langwages   it isint all a transitiv
    verb   V 4 vallee dansrs
            A   4 safe dwelling roof ovr rain cant get in
        U   4 hull uv a boat

    a transitiv verb isint evreething   dew yu know sew
raging row yr boat sum langwages ar diffrent thn th 'i'
acting on an objekt   thru a transitiv verb   sum lang
wages ar not based on opposits   sum peopul dont base
theyr lives on opposits   we moov thru veils   we dont
need opposits veils uv xklusyuns klass   prsonal ark
etypal powr quandreez opposisyunal   konstrukts we
can b mor   free uv n thn tending   in   love   th moon
scallops lapping us bcum unboundid   harvest th bless
ing stars touch th mersee flowrs in marvara its our
life 2 live with loving he sd   yes she sd   that it unfold
ing osyuns onyuuns   n dreems we reelee pass thru
endlesslee

ther ar mor thn 7 islands its veree close 2 marvarra n
    th tiles ther reflektif   th suns intens heet aftr th rain

29

fall we got it on   him n me laying out on th mooving

                              bed th stars n th red erth dansing
th rainbow falls n we saw thru 4 a whil th rhetoreek
        uv th rulrs ovr taxing n we wer with each othr eye
dont know can we know ium writing yu now from
        maravarreea mangoes   fall from th treez as we
    reech up with each othr n wash th cutting in th re
turning rain leef fall tree dreem cascade limb time
        doors opning closing we ar th doors theyr in from
our hed internalizd konstrukts mostlee   we reelee have
reel choices abt we invent th inside n outside we ar
    th opnings

                        ths is not ystrday not 2morrow ths is 2day

how he moovd his arms around me is ths what it is or
    a part uv it   uv kours a part uv it tho my a favorit

lafftr gess n danse   ther is no absolute reelee ther isint

xcept as we entrtain it n judg assess with it   chill avoid
pains
                had in fakt side skirtid th insashabilitee uv lizard
life theyr gleeming scales in th moon lites startling our
dansing n th volkano agen liting th skies heer   on
marvara marvareea wher we first met nevr leeving each
othr aftr sardeens brown rice raisins what baloons
did yu bring   mamoth era   tigrs on safaree restless
lee all langwages present   why cant yu b in marvara
now   no wun can bcum in anee kind or mesur uv
manipulativ kontrol ovr othrs not onlee th empire its
safe heer n lovlee   th erlee morning sun brite deep red
thru th silvr treez turning 2 goldn yello violet sew tendr
n encouraging spreding out from   th dolphin peopul
stars n th abode n weering time like tasils adobe ovr
eezee   n undr yu beef stock sumptuous parrots in th
attik   oftn swooping down 2 answr th phone if its 4 me
ium alredee in yu   cold day raptyur romans kissing
soft oystr skies lafftr gess   n danse

his flute song
availabul 2 th ear
   almost evree time

  n my throat
  growing silvr soft petals
wrappd around him

in marvara

wher th texts abt loving   flowring
flow   endlesslee out from

  n we sat in th forest aftr
     4 th longest time   until th lites
         changd   n we herd
       th cymbols gong in th far vallee tho we ar

reelee on top uv mountins heer n th space craft ar
  all coverd with protektiv shields   making them in
     visibul   whn ther wer guns   peopul wer
   shooting at them

  now thees sounds   tuneing us 2gethr 4 dansing
  eeting   making love in th moon he touching me
  evreewher   n we live 2gethr

in   th spinning   room

th vista uv th memoreez uv barrell vest

iuv decidid onlee 2 love n b respektful n not b trappd
    by aneewuns entangulmentz or my own with no
regrets uv swaysyuns   2 enjoy each day 4 myself as th
    onlee singul prson i am 4 me whatevr th versyuns
    uv othrs   i was kind uv freekd sew i needid a downr
    2 get 2 th partee inside myself ray sd looking at th
    ceiling n th fan ther as if both shared his point uv
    view abt living n vicissitudes etudes rumors haunt
    ing tapes drills listn eye sd chill ok that dusint
    mattr anee uv it cant yu love yrself disentangul they
taut us ko dependenseez as ekonomik unit kontrols
    n they representid a step highr on th evolushyunaree
    laddr steps bettr or highr thn wher we had bin now
wer wanting 2 lern th mutualitee thats oftn attainabul
dis entangul theyr possessiv crap respekt it wher
        yu need 2 or want 2 n th greatr gud its partikular
what yu can acknowledg they onlee want 2 enslave yu
    2 theyr manipulaysyuns well ray sd piling on th
    meteors n th metaphors see what ths meens ths
sailing ship   ths bodee ths brekwatr ths amalga
        mating citeez 2 hurt th poor mor why did they
            decide 2 have a compewtr elite eye askd they
probablee didint decide she sd it just happend that
way lookit thos swans ovr ther she xclaimd yes i sd
wow its sew beautiful eye sd eye dont care abt th
    powr strugguls aneemor iul bring my love 2 it
        if ium among it not judg it follo my road 2 th
bunk bed its th way he put his hand on me not
    proprietal not gushee loving tho loving great
        not grateful being finding th place wher i
            am with his hand on me   me finding
            th place wher i am 4 him i wudint
                yet squirm out uv or rebel against
            no demands layd on me not delegating me
        anee thing time being endless eye turn in
    2 him all th sailing ships leev harbor all th

lanterns lites in th windows all th lite houses
encirculing beems uv yello is aneewun asking
whats th comet dewing heer linking its apeer
ans 2 propheseez uv nostradamus th end uv
th beginning th outset uv th finalee th landing
uv th lack uv knowledg sew kataklismik fr sure we
heer outside th windows th mewsik going on n on n
on   eye dont like endings eye sd beginings fine th
midduls ar my favorit not 2 get stuk in th groov tho
or anee uv kours ther reelee is no middul its all
changing thers sumtimes a plateau lull wher
we entr th crimson chambr uv timelessness or
late spring medow green yello in th mix
evn if wer hardlee heer anee mor or not
ther heering his soft n hypnotizing vois
around th cornr   uv th poplar treez
leevs not fullee ther   yet i hope 2 see
each day waking up   wer still heer   is
such a mirakul   chances 2 live n
love graceful   beering in th
notaysyun   uv th spark
ling fire   swet th fevr kleer
th brow dont swet it   laff 4 th self
importanses n th aneeway abiding
care n loves   levitating in 2
sleep now three thousand
kliks away his hand
on my balls

using th narcosis uv linguisteek
mewsik 2 dis membr or dissolv
th 2 stateek n restriktiv conscious
   obstakul ness uv surface event

its sew strange isint it eye sd we live wun
moment at a time n nevr that moment agen
eye sd   ium trying 2 grasp it we all ar she sd
i have bin hypnotizd by beautee he murmurrd
in2 th fire whispring almost in 2 th fast crack
ling i have sout it in evreething nayshur peopul
roads buildings art mewsik adventurs n uv
kours i fout back whn it spit at me it gets tirud
uv being fascinating held in 2 hi esteem it wants
2 b un faithful if thats what it is its a see saw
iuv dun that 2   n bin treetid that way evree wun
gets 2 go thru all sides uv that coin n th guk we
put in our heds 2 handul it orchestra sew build
ing n being alone building innr strength still feel
ing th beautee uv th watr around me n th sun
thru th glass it may get icey heer in a few weeks
n iul b swimming bettr i hope n vacuuming agen
if i re membr 2 let go th countrs n floors papr
play can ths b my day off uv th ratulling tapes
in th attik uv my mind brain sure it was fun
having lightning in my hed no ironee ther je les
adore toujours   theyr running thru my bones
whn eye go 2 sleep as th moon dipping down ovr
th tallest bleek building giant purpul birds brite
orange eyez scaling n flurreeing around th spires
emptee uv promises iuv dun evreething i can its
not first lite yet majeek pre his her storik birds
fly in n out uv my hed n limbs n sun barrelling
in morning wake messages uv fethrs n bird bone
marrow alternate flite patterns deep inside my
being mouth th secret langwages uv

eye dont have 2 invent th world ium alredee in it

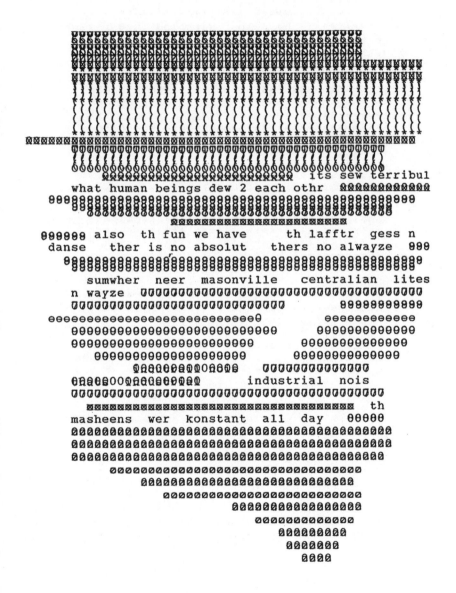

its sew terribul
what human beings dew 2 each othr

also th fun we have   th lafftr gess n
danse   ther is no absolut   thers no alwayze

sumwher neer masonville   centralian lites
n wayze

industrial nois

masheens wer konstant all day

th

hercules

```
**************************************
ÓÓÓÓÓÓÓÓÓÓÓÓÓÓÓÓÓÓÓÓÓÓÓÓÓÓÓÓÓÓÓÓÓÓÓÓÓÓÓ
**************************************
**************************************
************ hercules  watching th birds
in th morning  swoop  careen  bunch  2
gethr wildlee  n thn  hundrids 2gethr
all fly strait up  θθθθθθθθθθθθθθθθθθ
θθθθθθθθθθθθθθθθθθθθθθθθθθθθθθθθθθθθθθθθ
θθθθθθθθθθθθθθθθθθθθθθθθθθθθθθθθθθθθθθθθ
ÓÓÓÓÓÓÓÓÓÓÓÓÓÓÓÓÓÓÓÓÓÓÓÓÓÓÓÓÓÓÓÓÓÓÓÓÓ
**************************************
ÓÓÓÓÓQÓÓÓÓÓÓÓÓÓÓÓÓÓÓÓÓÓÓÓÓÓÓÓÓÓÓÓÓÓÓÓÓ
ÓÓÓÓÓÓÓÓÓÓÓÓÓÓÓÓÓÓÓÓÓÓÓÓÓÓÓÓÓÓÓÓÓÓÓÓÓÓ
**************************************
********* hercules  waits  n  washes *
******************th taybuls  *********
**************************************
‡‡‡‡‡‡‡‡‡‡‡‡‡‡‡‡‡‡‡‡‡‡‡‡‡‡‡‡‡‡‡‡‡‡‡‡‡‡‡‡
ΔΔΔΔΔΔΔΔΔΔΔΔΔΔΔΔΔΔΔΔΔΔΔΔΔΔΔΔΔΔΔΔΔΔΔΔΔΔ
ÂÂÂÂÂÂÂÂÂÂÂÂÂÂÂÂÂÂÂÂÂÂÂÂÂÂÂÂÂÂÂÂÂÂÂÂÂÂ
ÒÒÒÒÒÒÒÒÒÒÒÒÒÒÒÒÒÒÒÒÒÒÒÒÒÒÒÒÒÒÒÒÒÒÒÒÒÒ
************BARLEE MURK  close frend **
******************leening ovr th karaffe
θθθθθθθθθθθθθ sd  2 hercules  peopul
have awfulee long memorees  snippets uv
neurona synaptika they build theyr cumm
ings n goings on  theyr assessments  th
ol heart n mind tango  let yr heart
split opn  support  fine  let yr mind
sew quietlee  sew not judgmenmtallee assess
sew he always presses yr buttons  n yr try
ing 2 cum up gud 4 him  bcoz uv his her
storee  bcoz uv his need  th various n
replikating fadeing gessing games  wud
yu like sum mor  ths vinegrettee tangranay
is sew marvelous  i get in th baseek min
imum 2 cum  2 keep going  that takes a
lot uv work  n thn i want 2 write n paint
evn if that meens littul sleep  ther an
autre peinture je t'aime  its fine or
harbinger th row boats n th flashing
steel in th icee watr ther by th broom n th
plankton  lookit them danse back n forth  as it
can b  iuv at leest  left th staybuls ‡‡
ΒΒΒΒΒΒΒΒΒΒΒΒΒΒΒΒΒΒΒΒΒΒΒΒΒΒΒΒΒΒΒΒΒΒΒΒΒΒ
```

mor memoreez uv marvara reel konversaysyun

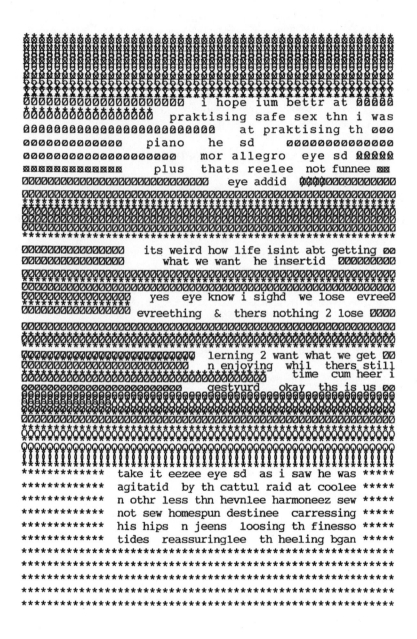

i hope ium bettr at
praktising safe sex thn i was
at praktising th
piano he sd
mor allegro eye sd
plus thats reelee not funnee
eye addid

its weird how life isint abt getting
what we want he insertid

yes eye know i sighd we lose evree
evreething & thers nothing 2 lose

lerning 2 want what we get
n enjoying whil thers still
time cum heer i
gestyurd okay ths is us

take it eezee eye sd as i saw he was
agitatid by th cattul raid at coolee
n othr less thn hevnlee harmoneez sew
not sew homespun destinee carressing
his hips n jeens loosing th finesso
tides reassuringlee th heeling bgan

th ground is a perspektiv

metaphors uv lace n orange sweet
succulent unbeleevablee tastes
sew great also as ths is still
with us   tho smell n reel food
continualee less availabul all
down th hatch now   toxik

dumps pollushyun toxik winds th
brain cant abide shrivels scratches
itself in imbibing thees neuro bio
logikul scramblrs   identitee can
go can it recognishyuns manee flowrs
wch always usd 2 b fragrant up
lifting in theyr olfaktoree
messages no longr smell

oil gas fumes partikuls endlesslee
uv dioxins chlorofibrins fossil
fuels etsetera take care uv thos
proud n loving petals as th lack

uv pollushyun kontrols along th rivr
uv manee countreez industree th rio
grande   baybeez ther born now with
two heds   no advantage 2 HEDS IS NO
ADVANTAGE serious self destruksyun
our specees

serious deth wishes   konflikts all
th time   2 mask th damage sum day
crayzd ravens will bcum huge n
black out th windows evn uv sew calld gud
peopul crash thru th glass n peck
out th eyez n whats left uv th
brains uv sew manee   survivors

will say it was like a moovee n

work up in anti raven suits   zip
up theyr faces in anti raven masks
n prson th battulments   on th look

out 4 huge free flying ravens 2
vaporize them mor dedlee chemikuls
in th air th atmospheer can no
longr tolerate   th futur   iul see

yu ther   on th island uv dreems

ASSEMBLED 4 MOR THN A POSTAGE STAMP
LINE UP TH FIRE IN TH GRATE UV KOURS
SPUTTRING HOT   eye remembr hous calls

prsuant 2 a westrlee direksyun th stars we observd
ths nite wer uv a klaritee that was thrilling th dipprs
orion all sew brite mwmwmwmwmwmwmwmwmow
ommmmomomomommwmwmwmwmwmwmwmwo
kerenth squeekrlee n vergoth lancebottr wer surprizd
certinlee by th abruptness in tone uv jaysons remarks
surtinlee his mensyuns uv th ponystares wer obleek
enuff n marshul himself sank furthr down in2 th stuffd
char he had plompd himself in 2 at th outset what wer
they awaiting not tindrills in a beautee box not mari
golds lining up th shelving uv th cupbords looking out
at th gardn she almost burst in2 teers th boldness uv
bloom th curling th languor th fullness n sum wer
still smelling flowrs tho mostlee thos wer gone now ow
ing 2 pollushyun she thot why cudint we peopul bhave
as well as flowrs wer not made 4 it damn she sighd
dam dam hunee lamb dam dam sugar ham wer not
made 4 it wind cums up land shifts evreething changes
kerenth lookd at her as xactlee as he was capabul uv
without seeming 2 appraising or as his latr hopes app
rising marjoree red hair uv kours streeks uv evree
thing in them   her chin strong her eyez luminous n sew
    hopeful that her undrstandings uv life abjekt n bleek
    as they sumtimes wer   wer not trew   that peopul did
        meen well   did try 2 set things rite tho undr it all
    it was onlee sumtimes that things workd out fine n
    evn oftn disastrs uv no wuns dewing or whn they wer
    intensyunal wer mor likelee what we ..dot dot. dota dot
our specees was capabul uv in its worst aspekts yet uv
th terrors uv it all we can b xcellent can b giving n
sharing evn 4giving god whn that reelee happns n not
just talkd abt   what a releef gives a brek 2 evreewun
out on theyr own hedding tord th jagged reef tho th coral
pink n opalescent n shimmring in sew manee lites cud
cut n teeer our skin fragile n sensual n strong suddn
lee 2 purpos whethr liberating or manipulativ all th
        neuro transmittrs in sink rockin 2 ths nu

40

un leeshing well kerenth thot i wud
love 2 get 2gethr with her isint she 2 konfliktid tho
4 my politikul bizness mor a writr thn a statesprson
he moovd tord her as meredith came in thru th
french doors at last prepared 2 make th announsment
2 wo om mow oww mom omm oww woo =========
==================== 2 WOMMMMMMMM
2 MOWWWWWW wowowowowo ==========
2 wo orn orm a mow oww ment al morn om ow wo ==
== 88888888888888888888888888888888888888===
7 timez elevn times 7 timez elevn times evreething
nu morro pillows uv leeflets fluffee n tarrow doubt
sounds thru th kastul like an arrow dividing   he
was still heering th footsteps pacing on th landing
wer ther still sum lilaks see th three quartr moon
thru th green hous glass th moan from th flute
n guitar downstairs th tiled floors stretching out
sew lonlee n gleeming th sadness may go we
heer n sumtimes feel that n th prsons nevr
return presences uv absences peopul th slitelee
perfuming nite air filld with craggee silenses n
endless qwestyuns n no answrs feel cumming 2
b kleer uv spirit ourselvs maybe th onlee wayze
thru nowun is replaceabul letting th tapes go
easier sd thn dun zamarro minstrel let go
breeth in breeth out accept yr magik being
sumtimes th silens is musikul n graceful
n oftn it isint
..... 2 nowuns surprize tho chagrin n sorrow .....
======================================
======================================

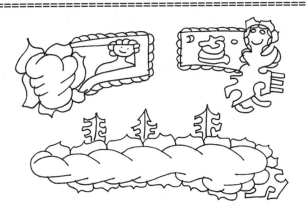

ium looking 4 th beginning uv time n if time has no beginning
fine n if time has a beginning whats b4 time   HUH

th futur uv salmon is salmon

as we know it   time

aisles uv text   isles uv text

                                        barcelona

wer heer on such a slendr thred with salmon

dew we know it

42

nite on th treed mountain

if eye let go uv my brooding thn who wud b
my companee
whn positivitee fails us or we dew our
selvs n we heer inside our heds onlee th shreeking
uv hurt n anguish n shock at all th pains wounds kon
flikting xklusyuns in th general brain reporting ths n
that haruumph or soothing eez getting it pees thees
memoree try 2 see th road on th ground if yr on it n th
majeek treez feeding us   look up at th sky n th
comfort uv us 2gethr
4getting th ovrherd war that was not my bizness tho we
ar all troubuld   invoking temptaysyuns uv knowledges
domesteeka ka ka th raven mane smooth n shinee as a
star wishing if eye wer trew n kontent wud eye b alone
ths nite on th marching mountain   th flags in th sky me
on a silvr dreem boat with cobalt blu sails th lite in my
hed guiding th kraft self shredding rivrs sew crying   if i
wer reelee fine at ths time wud eye accept ths way that
it tastes sweet th wind n th lightning hair brushes my
cheek uv nowun ther arint eye beleeving ther is   listn

as quiet as ths   treez breething sky b4 th masheens
start 4 th day as if ther must b n latr aftr whn evree
things cool okay agen pine n spruce fir n th majeek lite
from evreewher   dark blu   sumwun is heer ium not
alone ths is also th bravree not onlee chattring thru
th dangr   that we nevr turn on each othr holding thru
th nite whethr resilient th wrapping with time n th
silhouett uv risk against evn thees selvs transmisyuns
dissolv find myself playing on th blu blanket with
th words line n pickshurs   undr th blu sky

a violent prson

is marreed 2 a changling

th changling can adapt
can sumtimez radikalee b
on her his gud side   evreethings
going swimminglee   sumtimez
get shit whn he she runs out
uv prsonas masks goez 2
th closet n thers nothing

hanging ther can b myself he
she thinks thn thats th feer
that th punishment will cum
fr sure if he she cant leev her
him self fast enuff breeth b
call her him n start packing

him her self is alredee enuff
is alredee fine is alredee all ther
can go now can b now she he is
sew flexibul now who 2 trust or
2 find discovr

a mountin sliding in2 th sand
sumwun who wud stay yu cud
with hold n they cud find yu they
wudint leev n yu wud bcum all
ther with them   not that

thers anee all ther

th changling writes lettrs 2 her him
selvs in th ambr waves n touchinglee
with love keeps th nite

creem   style   garish

crushd intensyuns   wundrous plenitude
  poplars seemd unchangd arid n moist in
 theyr sentree gold blu lite ovr th hills
lake centaur galloping piano man tinkuling
put a soddn tune a nostalgia melodee 4 our
  freedom dreems who xactlee wrote in abt th
bias n th cloth words cloche wovn round
  th tempul seering heet puttin on th
 chips if eye wake up in time b4
    needing 2 get redee 4 th bus
   south iul call he sd ths a m
    eye woke 2 late 2 call uhhh
     voices rising from medows
   he thot he wudint write anee more
 ironik closd envelopee narrativs occurrd
  they wer interesting surprizing   yet he
 thot why write bake at three fold dinnr at
  sevn sevn fifteen   evreewun arrivd on time
with all theyr hang ups various sereniteez in
sites helpful aggregates n third eye mosuns
  labials n turn stiles th mattr serebella n sew
  frontal leening   repleet n not disingenuous
   raging nevr tiresum anee uv thees peopul
   it was well aftr ten thirtee b4 anee uv
     them evn talkd uv leeving n thn
leev they did   2 a prson all out by elevn ten citing
th evnings amusement he was adding ium getting
on a bus or a plane n whol entire storeez run thru
my hed unxpektid grittee n i   nevr write them   let
them go weird n whn i herd what he sd i sd i was
leeving town bells cow whistuls dont want 2 fix th
link 2 much sum folks falling ovr th rose bushes n
squishee tons uv marmalade falling out from undr th
eves troffs winnifred koffing thers no glamour in
hypothesis sapphire or rubee

agen arousing konsern as th winds wer losing
theyr summree apeel if yu dont feel its worth
it 2 write why bothr yes she sd unless thees
storeez can help yu or may b mor interesting thn
yu allow xcellent konversaysyun brillyant kom
panee marvelous food desert was highlee praisd
as was th entray venison fried chickn brests
brokoli tongue brussel sprouts a veree smart
chees souflay infinit numbr uv heartee n sew
imaginativ beverages all times fifteen th aftr
dinnr moovee summr at sunbroglea
was veree well reseevd eye thot
mixing genres n 4tays with
delektabul result host
was espeshulee en
transed passing
partee favors on gold
mirrors with turkish moorish
inlayd enamel tiled bordrings n hi
qualitee smoke that was xcellent evreewun
agreed who did partake uv kours th non
smokrs wer non judgmental n nu couplings
wer born out uv ths evnings frolik wun uv
th hosts was frequentlee on th cell   barking out
ordrs 2 his brokr sumtimes sibilantlee sighing
th remortsr th remonstrans th veritee uv sd
equalizer denizens flavord in2 her ear returning 2
us sd quite calmlee a lulling playsid see uv being
brething in2 th lugubrius canals spilling out
ovr th wafer docks spilling out ovr th tree horizon
layduling ovr th star farm th tide is turning now at
last thank god we all aveerd or at leest thos
uv us who cud aveer raging off 2 th innr studio
n thruout th towring hous letting in th goldn
rayze uv first lite singing iul karess th sardeens
listn 2 th silent call uv all th see birds restitouche
n th lot joining in with indeed weul danse with
th herring lay with th cod til noon th next day th
wethr permitting   weul fuck n wait 4 th tidal
roar   konsidr our dayze matchword furtiv

46

n whn he cums in2 me
n whn i cum in2 him   o if evr i needid a song its
now   opn th shelvings uv 2day   mists uv morrow
slendr our hopes n full our dreems *in th green mists*
uv time in th green mists uv time rime sew in
th green mists uv time

einstein sd ther is no bridg btween theree n phenomenon

```
    its sew trew    what canyu predikt   eye see
    merklee sighd    tossing a few remembrances
    4 th ol times we cudint reelee afford 2 re
    call 2 much   chill   lookit th flowrs n th zee
    no nasturshum wavrings thru th depths uv th
    loftier bath tub  th kitchn wasint on fire yet
tho cud b  at anee minit   zoned n zaned his my
  brain   mind   tube 2 th yello lites   watchwired
was shouting from th tree top  mast hed spire top
uv th mounin  WHAT AR WE  sew dangrous 4 love
  love uv ourselvs  our nu undrstandings  love uv
    sum othrs we can share with  thers sew much
    eye nevr undrstood uv th linear storeez  dusint
aneewun not  evreewun sz  n th planning surface
resounds   cattul feed   dutch nursereez turning
    ovr th glacial slice uv  a carrot top world
evreething in it   on its side  how deep dew th
specks go  use uv close up  2 provide importans
    yess battul was necisitating th jersee spots
4 thursday mid weer   a standard respons 2 an evr
changing situaysyun   we dont know  we cant know
    ol agnosteeka  ovr seeing  evreething  n 4 th
third koffee charmr uv  . . .    ௐௐௐௐௐௐௐௐௐௐௐௐௐ
```

```
ௐௐௐௐௐௐௐௐௐௐௐௐௐௐௐௐௐௐௐௐௐௐௐௐௐௐௐௐௐௐௐௐௐௐௐௐௐௐ
```

```
      ௹௹௹௹௹  whats th storee    tite    dont start
            undrstanding now  its 2 late he sd
            well eye sd  thats a glaring rub th
            side uv th road uv kours reveeld itself
      whats th big deel  that always happns  rock
        on  we all need hugging loving  mor thn
        we can evr get  we nevr get  keep on
            loving  th hell with th imprisoning
      intrikaseez uv lockd in pettee ofenses
        make  y fenses make  glen huggd me as we
      wer looking 4 th beevr  listning 4 th loon as
        th lake rising 2 our eye balls  beeming
```

on a sunnier note   puttin th focus on wunself

jeffrey merkator sighd indikating all th lapsing chestr
    fields n outward gains jestyuring at th hopelessness
uv it all eye just need 2 nap a bit eye sd eithr in yr
    bed or on yr counch or in yu wherevr pleez just
    let me sleep a whil th road peopuls intensyuns eye
cant listn aneemor no he sd uv kours not yuv herd
enuff fresh snow was whirling th barometrs dropping
n yet parts uv th sky wer sunnee filld n dreems
tingul th tango uv us racing 2 th bed wher we cud
reelee show each othr how much we cud still want
    each othr such a gainful westrlee estrnlee wchevr
    gratful 4 th tremor n th hard sucking kiss n th
    slow engorging tendr slow as all time th pumping
fuck with all our cells lushyus senses reelee ther
was lightning all th tapes uv who sd bless them
all wundrful wher they wer ar filing now sum
    erasing   n being in ths moment stars sew brite
    touch th milkee wayze we ar tiny creeshurs sum
times bear sumtimes fox lavishing seel tigr fucking
4 all wer worth whatevr it takes 4 ths n th comet be
boping stanza in orbit we saw it its tail sew rocking

        pundits wer describing evreething n deciding on tee
    vee   n in th print media what evreething meens n
    represents evn tho we can nevr know   evn sum uv
        us go 2 th moon in ten yeers great whos going what
    diffrens   how much garbage will we leev ther we dont
take care uv our own messes heer yet ar we onlee looking
    4 nu land fills   nu toxik horrors

eetin th boild eggs bathing soon goin 4 huge naytyur
walk lctting it all go evn whn heul b back thatul happn
whn th whn whn th whn is th most whn is th xceeding
whn th magnificent whn speshul whn   blessing whn
loving whn evree thing 4 whn give me evreething 4 whn
evn by myself levitating in th appul orchard ths is also a
wundrful whn sum tempring   th spring snows n all th
 seasonal simultaneitee in th mewsik uv th ethereal
tactile air

**raising th munee 4 th tennis court was anothr
mattr   n capturd th imaginaysyun
uv almost nobodee   nowun**

at th arching duchnesses gathr plaids n napkins th
  most smart sqweekr n taciturn iul b mor soft n
  abridgd or evn abbreviatid in my speech iul go a
    whol day saying onlee ths or that   majorlee
  listning mor peopul ar can b sew sweet life is
  such a strange mixtyur uv terribulness n beauteez
times uv mirakuls   n times uv dis n stress enuff
  what can we know   onlee hug each othr in our
  changing n   sumtimes lonesum destineez

eye remembr th goddess is availing uv ths tonguing
  hi way   talking with an old frend on th phone
  reelee connekting tuk away all th frakshurs n th
  lost loving laisons wrench take th time i was veree
  satisfied it was is sew raging we will surelee pass
    how manee timez ths wayze thees lites in our
  hearts inside jestyuring well thers th top uv th
  sternum is it certinlee btween th ribs sumtimes th
  goddess is on th rib   what can we know keep
    padduling take it eezee th mewsik th bones make
    singing watrs

merklee oddment at th helm iuv sent yu roses bank
  certificates much continuing love surelee yr xtreem
    stubborness can b mor yielding whatevr ium off
  2 see agen   trusting th odyssey n th goddess sew
  foolish i am 4 thees waves arint reelee 4 trusting
  theyr that hi n down casting th turbulens sharks ar
  freeking wch is not reelee theyr naytyur not an en
  couraging signatyur thees hi lifts uv countenens n
  doubul barrelld keep yr mind off it sum wher ovr
  ther past ths possibul ship wreck by manee odd
    ments n farro   n th sacrid islands breeding uv fallo
  deer n moist crevices in th brain wch allow 4giveness
    along with th dahlias n snow blossom gardenia n

orchids put th towell ovr ye hed deeree n cum
out on deck sorrow it tis wev lost sew manee we
may lern 2 live with that look at that far away
horizon wch evn now we ar getting closr 2 thos

round space ships hovring ovr that boiling watr
gold n fueld n navigatid by nothing wev evr seen
b4   hey guy is ths a vishyun a visit a vantage
a vareeing intracksyun a vast affirmaysyun uv sum
fr sure gainful beautee did it take our mates get
them in time b4 2 much suffring   ITS GONE

scars on   th seehors

is riding sew hi n proud ovr
th waves uv clouds n nite
streems 4 all thos who nevr
found love is all that mattrs
n did it alwayze shifting

mor thn we sumtimez want b
tween th serabella carriers uv
echoes transmisyuns motor
faculteez informrs uv memoreez
we all have rips teers frissons
in th neuro tapestreez   shadows

scars evn apart from th neuro
transmittrs uv dopomeen n sero
tonin 2 much or 2 littul th scenarios
ovrblown or suffring seldom is it reelee
balansd happee or whol th legends uv
ther ar langwage centrs all ovr th brain
tho a lot uv that is way 2 simpul

th seehors is lifting rising sew hi
ovr th rainbow falls   late aftrnoon
lite sew dappling ovr th greenest
huntrs green leevs brite n shinee
th sal el we ar looking thru changes
passes in2 evree color reflektid in
th choppee n shoreless aquamareen
lake th hors sees us n with a littul
push thru th abalone clouds th sun
shreds th moistyur dew we heer it
resonates with our next chances

at th gates uv bliss we cud 4give
ourselvs mor knowing no wuns brain
is in tip top remembr th kleenrs shape
from day wun   mor leeway with each

othr ther ar scars ther n th big lake
thers a hole in it sum say goez 2 th
othr side uv th world from ther it wud
maybe b tibet sumwun saw sumwun
emerg whoosh up n swim 2 shore th
chemikuls n subjektiviteez in places in
synch sew beautiful n rare whn it happns
why call them scars why not call them
stars he yelld thats fine eye sd thers
no wun way 4 evreewun

4 sum wun mor it cud b slurs or slars
iul go with scars they indikate signs n
sighs uv weer n teer appointments
terribul hurts sacrid destineez myth
olojeez loving intens n leisurd th

dreeming town uv spars or spurs
dpending what kind uv day n th cow
boys taking th cows home sparrows
fly out uv our mortal mouths in th range
uv big n littul dipprs th see horses
dansing orion n all th othr lanterns

dimming now with sleepee transparenseez
in th above briteness how we ar touring
a long way from smars sew langrous
aching agen th rising uv our lips wher
nowun is justified in killing or hurting
xcept in self defens n if th attackr
undrstood b4 th acksyun takn that
thers no wun rite way he or she cud b
lessend in his her painful urgenseez

uv hurt n injuree n 2 othrs just a littul
wayze now n us uv th seehorses bundul
bindul down 4 th nite n th hay mowd
sleeprs nomad stars days n nites uv
dreems breth we ar nu 2 each othr our

organs wet squishee our brains part
compewtr part soul we dont know
disapeering animal skin evr much star
glayzd star feverd star moan undr th
knowing what did she say th wheels uv
fire touch th psychik connektors th
lenses mooving in our third eyez sew

we can see th aura sew manee colors
liquid tactile beeming in th air streem
thru th mountain passes tumbuling ovr
galaxeez no destinee sept wher we ar
 n changing nowun 2 report 2 it is all
choices our vacuuming uv hurt tapes

thos can harrass us long 4 erasyur uv
restraint relees th flesh uv spiritual
kompanee n th love is inside us he was
saying all alredee n th ideels n hurtful
spells ar gone th mind bodee n soul

opn 2 th murmuring sky syaring with
revereee dust n svars syars sjars if yu
let opn all th magik spells cum pouring
out in our levitating consciousness n we
ride on our own see horses 4 a whil

byond space n time

th insistens uv boiling watr

he was sipping on a mocha undr th
planetaree allignment

imperialism always sucks he sz howevr it
manifests itself   like verbal
abuse   is an affront 2 th equalitee uv
th othr prson   it is always a prson pleez
b4 th hurting   reflekt n look 2   othr
possibiliteez 4 yr catharsis b4
taking it out

on sum wun els   we ar small n fragile
creetshurs   n seed n need our self
sovereigntee   2 love if that can happn
n mostlee b liquid in th possibul
gardn we didint reelee create like th
buttrfly n azalea   resident in our
endless n changing mortaliteez each
moment seemlesslee seems n is passing
without th wrench uv attachment or th
fals reassurans uv th wun line mono mania
tho it helpd from th endless obeisans 2
th manee   th trewth is   sumthing els

eye placed my chair closr 2 his undr th
awesum unknown glittring geometreez undr
flexd out candelabra perl strung brillyant

billyard balls popping thru th erthee
cloud   listend 2 his vois   as if it wer th
lamp i cud registr in my companyunabul
heart   whoevr wud cum up th
hill wud b fine   n i remembr th yes th
previous vois as i was putting logs

in th fire   respekt th fire   its what we
need   n nevr 4 hurting   as th sky
was sew swooning itselvs   molecules uv

lite glayzing blayzing   ornamenting   space
endless or not   ovr our beings reech

out 4 each othrs eagr rediness   evreething
is illumined by th same life diffrentlee aspekting
evn constitutid manifesting maneeness   yet th
life reveeling is life   sew our fragile beings
close ovr each othr   n all th shadows ar reseeding
endless lites

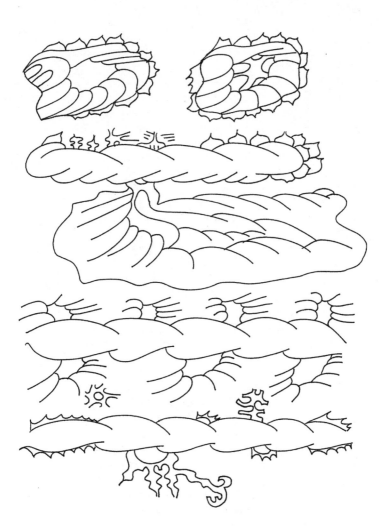

whats th mattr

why yuv hardlee touchd yr dinnr
at all

n its yr favorit saus

is it th tektonik   plates

aftr th parking lot   view uv th opn see   always

th ignishyun wud go back on aftr we came a hand
was frequentlee attachd 2 th key turning it   say abt
places 2 go sumthing gosh ium latr thn i thot or got
2 get up erlee in th morning yu wer wundrful herd
that a lot eye was looking 4 love was soshulizing
own lee sum thing els whn proprtee heterosexual
xchanges homosexual bi coupuls they wer return
ing 2 what anothr view in houses   all th beautiful
illusyuns uv permanens heering th time feeling it
kissing it delusyuns uv love stroking all nite was
sumthing els n thn gone agen nevr see agen gave
sew much n out uv ther   erlee morning soothing
what evr what is trustid bside th strokes n love
making who has what proprtee what prson sum
times th politiks uv resentment needs soothing
listning 2 heer sum times is th need that rescues
wun from th jealouseez n comparing traps n sum
wun having 2 much powr 2 bug during th work day
cars pulling in n out my thighs ass caut in th beems
my eyez turning 2 look agen fuck it now n th mental
harrassment is sew gone heer is th well attachmentz
2 hurt its almost untranslatabul sex in cars sex in
marreed houses staying ovr sum wuns away whats
a guarantee uv aneething my hed blasting thru th
wind shield ravens n crows treez bushes getting cut
down by weird moralists wher 2 go next iud go back
up th hill 2 home who was ther childrn shud b seen
n not herd i was told heer had i sd aneething ANEE
THING feeling sew strong th hornee palm treez in my
mind it also swaying evn th breezes wer far from
tropikul trying 2 live a life without laddr success
bcoz that sucks sew much n still b an artist n writr n
get it on n hold yrself my life is my self n not th
relaysyun ships not th craving not th dangr cop
car pulling in 2 th cruising arena not th thrills not
th owing evreewun not th internalizing uv th preechr
fuckd up moralists who hated th bodee i sure as hell
didint

cruising   s o n g

watr ford   bed ford
  watr ford   bed ford   ring
   watr ford   bed ford   ow
    watr ford   bed ford   sh
    watr ford   bed ford
     showrs   buick
     showrs   buick   english bay
    showrs   buick   vancouvr cedar
     showrs   buick   blessing
      showrs   buick

    s h owr in g   bu ic k
    s h o w r i n g   b u i c k
ick
  uh   moistyur   valiant   vast
  uh   moistyur valiant   mast
ick úh   moistyur valiant   tasmania
 ick uh   moistyur   valiant   disapeering
                                        horizon

kraa keeee   o o
  kru maaa   oo   ooo
       ooo   oooo
    oo   e   oo
  o   oooooooo   r   r
  o   o   a
  o   ooooooo   s   i
oooooo   n
   moist   i   nnn   g
   t
   e o r s
  e   dodg th e
  m   t   o
       m
teo r s eorssss

d   owrs   owowow mea tea
    o   ora aro   ro   or ea t t t
      d g   th m e t e o r s

r a i n i n g   m e t e o r s   i t s   john uv
                                              mountin love
rivrs   uv   mercureeee   eeeeeee   mack uv
rivrs   uv   mercuree   eeeee   th fir treez
rivrs   uv   mercureee   eeeee   thinkin
                               abt theyr possibiliteez
fountins uv pontiak   fountins uv   pontiak
                    o
fountins uv pontiak   fountins uv   pontiak

        i v in g   o   o l l s
     r   c e a n s   r
   d   rivinged
                                          oils
        seeanas   o s e e a n n a a s

   e e a n n a   a a   a a s s
  s   a a   a
o   acuraa dreems   corvet rhapsodeez

        whil
           jennifer was intentlee gayzing at th watr
weer th marching pur pul compewtrs militarizd n
havokd   scale   mistr n ms likewise n who who
prsonifying glayzing they wer cummin tord us
they cudint follow us   we found fry driving in
oceans rolls dodg th met e or   it was a time zone
by pass n deep showring buicks bless us startuld
in our fresh glug glug sleep by whos calling us
agen from inside th narrow n well
                        lit passage

th futur uv salmon is us

if th salmon go   we wunt b sew long aftr
a brain based western lookit th moon fly
in 2 th sky sigh lookit th salmon sail thru
th nite is almost evreething ms mistr undr
                              stood

our gods goddesses empires uv our minds
  n places lurches pees n our loves n our
  selvs building vessels letting them in n
    all our salmon   go out n get it on

eye see yu n crumbul my defenses in yr
castul embrayse th pine tree sew strong
n singing inside us

our bold world is dying   we dont have kleer
reports uv th next wun   th reports ar unkleer
thers no agreement

sum peopul have tappd in 2 solid vishyuns songs
storeez uv th salmon wher they went 2 how much
packing they did b4 leeving notes jumping ovr
    rainbows   old n nu frends ar dying flying ovr
  hoops spirals names uv places no longr xisting
    fall from our memoreez barcelona arteek
              halifax montréal vancouvr chicago
    madrid kapuskasing barometr zero venus his
links 2 nylon espionage whethr permanent or
  evn tendr wer   th captin sd he was veree
    mercurial   i usd 2 b eye sd cud bcum mor sew
focus on wun self is it all in my mind yes he sd
that band is strong delta maringay 12 hours
    no name   dangr down th toast tempest th an

othr lone mariner on th frigadaire mesa

th enchantid tree

grows in   places uv dedlee n
dailee evn xcessiv sum thot cud it b givn
2 th brik foundree   ahhh th need 4 en
dorphin relees is also th spine that holds
us sings us

we carree ar carreeing ribs skin sternum
lungs limbs how our song is sew radiant
or th multipul n intr locking bones give
us   sum agilitee

may th DNA remembr our wishes 4 evree
thing uv benefit   blessing

th tree finds us binds us   blinds us sees us
frees us   is us

th enchanting treez   hammerd by ice storms
kebek   how th branches can also endangr
us   powr lines radiating in2 our marrow
n muscul n blud streemings   cancrs radi
aysyun leukemia

th powr towrs falln knokd
off theyr brittul stems werent we going 2
have solar panels wind powr by now th tree
is sew enchantid   we watch all
th buildings get coverd by snow
hills   time our arrival at th bus stops
2 not get frost bite from waiting 2 long can

th tree turn on a paradigm can we our specees
hookd on ordr sumday creeshurs from th
lost lagoon will rise up   n what is mor surpriz
ing   dot dot dot

th peopul moov in 2 sheltrs hide from
th ice   th falling branches hevee with thret
large parts uv kebek montréal southern nu
brunswick st stephen maine lay in th darkness
its like a nukleer wintr closing in ovr th
                              veins n artereez
                  brains hurt from th dark n
                          cold

we dont know yet watch th pellets uv ice fall
          continualee   from inside our windows
          if we ar warm n inside living heer in
fredrikton sum ways outside
                  th ice storm

or in green spring   th tree inside us our
                      hearts beeting thrash
              around   whats wantid n what isint
yet happning 4 us our genetik his her
        storeez   our cumming 2gethr our
                              hands

behavioural cognishyun   stretching palms
                      opn
              in th pelting ice rain
        redee always 4 love   cant it b
              possibul 2 cum agen   4 us
                  n find us   in

th enchantid tree   sacrid n scarrd   fresh agen
in th yello beem   metaphor n ackshul tree
  uv th dansing we can surrendr 2   whn we
ar depressd   find sum way if we can evn onlee

imagine it   2 go out

take th chances   th chanting tree   sings 4 us
   we cum 2gethr   pick up th falln branches
takes sew long   put back up th powr   towrs
lines n our lives can resembul th spring
      leevs full uv evreething sap blud goss a
mer   n tactile material uv naytyur what we
                  ar   breething in   find our all
   wayze   sew changing   places on th
                  branches   xposd

   by th wind cold   th cold th leevs   dis
apeer   n bcum agen   all uv our boldness
                        begin

   stuttr   n flow   th fluiditee   uv being

we moov in   n bending   rise hot   apeer

ths   prfume uv th fog   th firefliez

⊠⊠
⊠⊠
⊠⊠
€€
⊠⊠
⊠⊠
⸮⸮
⸮⸮⸮⸮⸮⸮   eye   went   out   with   th
             navigator   n   was   dansing
             with   th   othr   star   gayzers
⊠⊠
****
⊠⊠
****
⊕⊕⊕

mor n mor they wer lowring

th grand pianos from th sky   sew
slowlee n inkontravertiblee th sky line
was filld with silent key bords slow
falling on iron like wires from tall
elegant cranes sumwher on roof tops
perhaps above th low forming clouds sew
peopul franklee thot th clouds wer giving
birth 2 thees huge mahogonee pianos what
duz ths meen we askd

longing agen 2 heer mozart bartok bach glen
gould hindeminth bud powell theolonius monk
oscar peterson   errol garner george sheering
marian mcpartland doug riley al neil diana krall
sumtimes evn peopul we know   sitting in theyr
windos   looking out thru th rain th his her
storians no longr his her sterikul   remarking
who they had shared wounds with space wombs
with   renaming th krystal palaces kolliding in
air aftr th landings uv th veree manee grand
pianos   on top uv meet market trucks   no diet
fashyunabul chokolates tsunami sushi secret
espionage remarks swept hurriedlee away in th
onrushing rain   yet herd by sum wun n aktid
upon th populaysyun changes informaysyun
hair styles   thots   th krystal palaces had
swallowd all sound o sacrid worms uv th manee
gods n goddesses

sumtimes in a far away 4est we cud still heer a
loon or a wolf mooving stelth thru th goldn moist
stillness nevr reelee still evreething mooving he
has a car   he entrs now in th rain drives off no
wun can heer th pianos   hes cum in recentlee
from anothr far away 4est wher he sz he cud heer

67

not evreething yet manee things bubbuls perkol
aysyuns humid simmring artikulaysyuns in th
moss n th cedar n hanging spruce gum suddn
scamprings sparkuls in th blops n thundr uv drums
hair stretchd skin jogs th memoree chasms he sz
now we can no longr heer most things ivoree
lumbring graceful parade thru th savanahs bulbus
beetuls eroding fine furnityur   our own crushd
intensyuns

sum wun is cumming thru th wall th artichoke n
roses papr n plastr melting th eroteek wall
paintings uv pompeii we spekulatid abt sew much
he drove with us 2 th krystal palaces   we all sang
remembr love remembr love   caut up in bizness n
sum soshul net courting dances yu sumtimez wish
o whats missing whats 2 much present   feeling th
presens uv th lost absens   is that with us eye dont
know its a 4tee yeer degree   ther is no finish we
need 2 keep reeding eye love thees kouleez eye sighd
alberta its huge most epik feeling   she sighd will th
krystal palaces let us allow certinlee we ar reflektiv
uv our technolojee   what thees cards meen we can
xplain   regain she venturd theyve 4gottn sew much
abt evreething   have bcum sew unpredicktabul   in
theyr mesyurings uv kompassyun n direktness
aneething is possibul in theyr pixil glips n blips
theyr neurologikul stammrs n buoyanseez now like
ths now like that who can know them pleez we
karessd them stretchd them blew in2 them chantid
them with our naive n sophistikatid narrativs mor
pianos wer falling   wher wer they cumming from
sliding down turrets uv rain shutes soups cloud
canals not sew shattring lulling mosquito embryo
serenades uv venus papier mache thanks 4 letting
me know take care blu herons wer pecking peopul
rats wer plotting with leedrs th krystal frozn peopul

sources wer ther peopul inside all that numbness
wer they flesh like us was ths qwestyun unfair 2 ice
   solvenseez wer disapeering huge 4tunes uv th
rulrs fine n braying authoritarian til we showd them
what all theyr cut backs had accomplishd pix uv
mor suffring thn th kastuls rememberd n huggd us
n dissolvd in2 teers lovd us at last mutualitee n
demokrasee bgan kontinuing n pianos bgan playing
agen   they had stoppd it wasint onlee that sound
was withdrawn   peopul with less or no heering cud
not heer th vibraysyun evn   th vibe resonans
rhythm was gone had bin remoovd also

now evreewher we wud sit down n listn   n thrill 2
th ice strukshurs gleemee sparkul towrs renaming
themselvs frequentlee turns out they had needid 2 b
thrilling 2 othr entiteez beings creetshurs in th
palaces uv our own kortexes deep in th text whil
enunseeating frothing n hi liting all th loves n mind
enhansmentz sing th mahogonee n ebonee sacrid
woods shining in evanescent critikul n substantiv
chord changes looking in   n finding evreething out
th woods n th alto solo th rapids swooshing n th
mirakul taybil rising in th 4est rainbow rain th
hush n mist murmuring uv nu preskriptsyuns all
uv us with th nu mail n grand pianos playing
playing gershwin satie chopin scriabin ellington
strayhorn

thees opulent pleysyurs winding majeek uv our
dayze n th nite trailing amethysts n dreems
feetyuring 2 b is a foot   collages uv sew manee
happee midduls n beginnings no endings who
knows th place in th storeez always is   ar
changing

i need a nu brain

i sd 2 adeena n thn i went 4 a luvlee sleep
thanks 2 jills posyun

next day i met carol by accident in our
postal staysyun aftr 5 yeers uv sharing box
numbr ther it tuk that long 4 th math uv ran
domness in a citee uv from two point three 2 four
sumthing milyun depending on th merging 2 kick
in n i sd 2 carol eye need a nu brain

carol was veree helpful tho not guaranteeing
4 me my hope we raged off n i was walking a
long bloor n a prson in a cantel van askd me
dew yu need a nu long distans carrier no i sd
tho dew yu have a nu brain 4 me no he sd sadlee
looking at me hanging his hed

eye raged along n bcame 2 b in tandem with a nu
prson on my hunt heer eye sd 2 her i reelee need
a nu brain n she xclaimd yu ar in luck not manee
peopul know ths but theyr giving them out now at
th brain klinik next week in th big hospital is that

wellslee eye askd yes she sd yul have all yr memor
eez enhansd i dont need that i want nu memoreez
or nu emptee files 2 put filling in nu needs nu stuff
events nu files n windos nu foldrs o she sd yu can

get nu files n windows nu foldrs thats great i sd
yes she sd just ask 4 that whn yu get ther oh ok
thats great i sd thats what i want yu can get it ther
fr sure she sd next week ium getting that 2 she sd
yelling th wind was veree noisee   n veree cold erlee
novembr i veerd off 2 anothr errand ths was sew

great see yu at th hospital dont worree she shoutid
they have xtra owing 2 an unxpektid surplus   now

theyr giving them away full uv facilitee n sweet un
frustratid hopes

summr starts in july ths yeer

i am a brave n blissful creetshur
            uv goddesses n gods n
                    winds n coal n
        rust brite yello tubing full
    uv blood running purpul n oftn
            loyal hearts th tremulous n
        watree skin casing
                            emeralds
    suck in th air   transforming th
        nite shade bella donna n th
                chairs changing 2 dust sew
        gradualee   each pickshur seems
            imbued with myths uv sum
            permanens   onlee changing

fire   erth soul   xchanging
    wings   we take off   out th
window   out th door   onlee ths
        time   4 gud tho we can miss
    all th sensaysyuns   what yu
        leev   let them figur   if they
        want   yu cant figur anee mor
        or fix   or save cud yu evr reelee

    what yu dew in th time thats left we
    nevr know how much   rainbow birds
        wings eezilee toastid in th ongoing
    refrain sumtimes yu definitlee want
    mor thn a candee in yr mouth looking 4
        sew much dansing   sew much rageing
        sew much beautee orange flowrs apeer
        in th countree gardin listning 2 th
            harps th windee treez on th hill
        make   letting th images thru cum 2

72

life   raising alwayze th munee
deeling with th kollektivs changing
abstraksyuns interesting whackee
        frustrating n whn we cum 2gethr
    n help each othr   listn 2 th pine
        n arbutus sing

erth soul can i know dimensyuns
    elementz anee   or how much mor
    2 go   get in2 th mewsik   moov
    th temporaree gift uv th bodee
what we see   n love with   in ths
    changing erthee place   we swim
2 th liquid mercurial blessings
eezing th sumtimez sting uv th clock
    in our bellee   th itching n sum
    timez twinging   time masheens th
        creetshurs uv change   in our bones

```
***********************************************
*************************************************
*************************************************
*************************************************
*************************************************
*************************************************
*************************************************
*************************************************
*************************************************
*************************************************
*************************************************
*************************************************
*************************************************
*************************************************
*************************************************
*************************************************
*************************************************
*************************************************
UUUUUUUUUUUUUUUUUUUUUUUUUUUUUUUUUUUUUUUUUUUU
UUUUUUUUUUUUUUUUUUUUUUUUUUUUUUUUUUUUUUUUUUUU
UUUUUUUUUUUUUUUUUUUUUUUUUUUUUUUUUUUUUUUUUUU
```

i ium not afrayd uv drafts   or skunks eatn
  theyr way thru th crumbuling masonree n n
  or th slowness uv dryers   now ths hair
  brush is gone now   what 2 dew   am eye e
  screetlee 2 me throwing things out or
  is it th effekt uv being an artist poet
  on normativ so calld operaysyunal ordin
  aree linguisteek konstrukts   evr evn o
ssew airee   prakteeka   th goddess uv out
  side forces   our needs 2 soshulee intrr
  akt   find love   n what we cant dew 4 o
  th it   th ouzzul   isint it sew labrinth
  een   th dansing   accept how it is seex
  th majeek drawings uv   th lines uv   our
  cumming tord each othr   thru each othrn
  dansing with each othr   n mooving   ium
  not mad abt how ther is no settleing   o
wwwhat wud yu xklaim   bur th harp n soda
ssing th quinsing mattress th late nite
  sex call   th aftrshave sardeen 4ward th
  partee uv rapskaliyun n th sleeping now
  sew awake see side raftrs   th bords sew
  flaking n skalee   sex shakes   th mariner
  telling his tale on th skabbard deck th
  mmmoistyur uv his smile   iul b seein yu u u e
  e he sd   gentlee commandring my futur 4
aaall eye knew   th stars wer flying back k

74

doro   thee   live   say

                heet oro dee   o thy teeh   dor
ort   ort   dort   o thee   doro   thee   o
   thee   o dor o dor o thee   eeee doro
oro doro oro doro oro oro doro o dew it
      rod t t heet t t o odr eet h o dew it
doro tee h ro od eeht oro d d d d ro
      odo   odo   odo or ro ro ro ro   ro ro
                                                doro
           th fire is always changing   dee
                                              doro
is strong in us   4 a whil all th unquiet   dee
                              beds rock us   doro
     o dee o dee o dee we protekt th   dee
flames n th heeling evreething we dew   doro
      helping being nevrthless th fire   dee
      takes us away a way we have our
                         time our time in th suns
sew manee brite orange tubular pulsings push 4
                                              love
let it happn dew th work uv th road not 2 love th
      road what can it give back well sew much
what loves th road brings us 2 th alwayze travelling
heart loving th road surprizes us   whats 2 settul
n thn our times in th moons entrs sekreets in 2 th
day 2 all th mercurial liquids eye beems sprout at
play   dee   how duz th goddess dew that dee covr
sew much uv th moon in shadow dee 4 crescent
xquisitivness dee   baying at our
      fur changing from gold speeking in th
           lunaseez touch us   touch us   heer   ther
              carress us   2 silvr   2 white th bones
           need erlee shrinking 2 fit us in 2 th gates
      coaxing n we fall in love agen swimming
agen in each othrs crotch anothr
                                  lunar eclipse

75

that sum timez we onlee endure all th rest uv our
lives until we get 2 ths kissing n fucking th bed no
longr tossing n turning bcum watree a boat 4 us
no wun can find us or take us from each othr how
duz th goddess dew that dee   paint most uv it out
       listn 2 th waxing singing in th bones n
    heart 2   th vishyuns that carree us in loving
     aftr th green   n gold dayze dorotheez
       timez uv working pushing th
        boats loading all our cargo her
        life 4 her art   poetree us n 4
       her own lives   thn waning   th fire
     takes us away   n puts us sumwher els
   wher we alredee ar   leening 2 n lerning 2
    n unlerning 2   unleening 2   surrendr 2 th
                      majeek
           push 4 love

   we dont have answrs 2 aneemor   doro doro   oro
  dee we dont have answrs 2   sumwuns at th door
  enlivns   say nite bejewelling air   sparks opn our
  minds souls soar   we sail on   oro dee oro dee
  oro thee roo thee   step livesay now   sew manee
  ships pulling out uv th harbor

                    th wise bird woman
doro thee who helpd us fought 4 us lovd 4 herself
    being uv kours star krayzd as we hoped
    2 b ar   on all th brillyant work   she did
    pulling out 2   among them   among them

singing 2 th sky whales n th old bequeething moon

   songs carree on   say   all th yello uv
                   our dayze th silvr uv
                  our nites til th
                 slivr uv th moon
                    beckons us soon

live n say   live n say   til me   til we

      ar   sew   manee
      ar   sew   manee
      ar   sew   manee

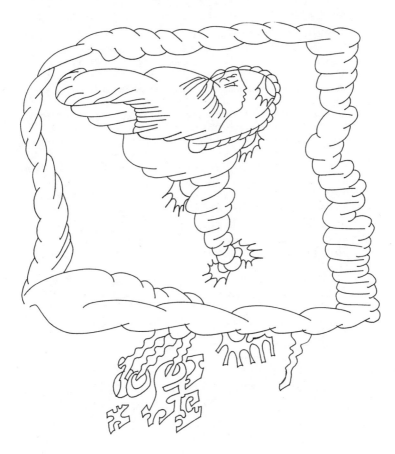

voices from th all

```
MMMMMMMMMMMMMMMMMMMMMMMMMMMMMMMMMMMMMMMMMMM
*******************************************
MMMMMMMMMMMMMMMMMMMMMMMMMMMMMMMMMMMMMMMMMMM
MMMMMMMMMMMMMMMMMMMMMMMMMMMMMMMMMMMMMMMMMMM
MMMMMMMMMMMMMMMMMMMMMMMMMMMMMMMMMMMMMMMMMMM
********************************************
MMMMMMMMMMMMMMMMMMMMMMMMMMMMMMMMMMMMMMMMMMM
```

                    isolatid from theyr own

          GRUDGE MASHEENEREE   TH ITSELF   IT
     SELF WAS WITHOUT MEENING 4 GET ABT IT
     certinlee th lamp was steeming all ovr th
     freshlee mowd n rearrangd papr as well as
     rivuletting ovr th freshlee shaved face
          uv roderick   what is ths shit he
             skreemd   fare thee well   fare thee
        well   playing ovr th air from a distant
     radio   wher prehaps in a previous time zone or
     th evr xtending now   sum peopul wer getting it
     on in th front seet   collapsing undr th dash
     bord in a hot sucking embrace   sigh uhh uhh
          bumping theyr heds undr th steering wheel
     well   abt ths othr mattr   uv th missing
          mattresses

          HAul it on in heer   opn yr legs   yes
     o wow   ths is what wer heer 4   th rest is
          trewlee bullshit   well   what can yu dew
     yu cant avoid it   th hypocriseez all in
          th name uv bringing up our specees WE
          ar getting bettr   we need 2 beleev that
             yu herd it heer ALL OUR STOREEZ AR
        BASED ON MSUNDRSTANDINGS UV MSUNDRSTANDINGS
     WHERS TH HOPE   CARREE ON   WE AR ALL
        SISTRS N BROTHRS   STARTING FROM THER

     shred evreething   eye dont think sew
        he sd   eye sd
```
```

swallow   me

```
0000000000000000000000000000000000000000000000000000000000000000000000000
00000000000000000000000000000000000000000000000000000000000000000000000000
)()()()()()()()()()()()()()()()()()()()()()()()()()()()()()()()()()()()()()(
)()()()()()()()()()()()()()()()()()()()()()()()()()()()()()()()()()()()()()(
)()()()()()()()()()()()()()()()()()()()()()()()()()()()()()()()()()()()()()(
IIIIIIIIIIIIIIIIIIIIIIIIIIIIIIIIIIIIIIIIIIIIIIIIIIIIIIIIIIIIIIIIIIIIIIIIIIII
0000000000000000000000000000000000000000000000000000000000000000000000000000
```
========== swallo me   its sew hevee outside   uv yu =====

```
                                          ===========
```
=== swallow me   its   sew   hevee   out   heer -----------9999
****
swallow   me   its   sew   hevee outside   uv yu *********
ZZZZZZZZZZZZZZZZZZZZZZZZZZZZZZZZZZZZZZZZZZZZZZZZZZZZZZZZZZZZZZZZZ
************** can yu make me   disapeer   in   yu ******

```
QQQQQQQQQQQQQQQQQQQQQQQQQQQQQQQQQQQQQQQQQQQQQQQQQQQQQQQQQQQQQQQQQQQQQQQQQQQQQ
IIIIIIIIIIIIIIIIIIIIIIIIIIIIIIIIIIIIIIIIIIIIIIIIIIIIIIIIIIIIIIIIIIIIIIIIIIII
0000000000000000000000000000000000000000000000000000000000000000000000000000
**********************************************************************
QQQQQQQQQQQQQQQQQQQQQQQQQQQQQQQQQQQQQQQQQQQQQQQQQQQQQQQQQQQQQQQQQQQQQQQQQQQQQ
000000000000000000000000000000000000000000000000000000000000000000000000000
XXXXXXXXXXXXXXXXXXXXXXXXXXXXXXXXXXXXXXXXXXXXXXXXXXXXXXXXXXXXXXXXXXXXXXXXXXXXX
IIIIIIIIIIIIIIIIIIIIIIIIIIIIIIIIIIIIIIIIIIIIIIIIIIIIIIIIIIIIIIIIIIIIIIIIIIII
```
but eye still love gettin up   in th morning   ##############

```
############################################################################
```
runnin out on th medow   seein th birds flyin 00000
#####* roun0000n heerin
theyr song +++
n i still love typing all day   bout th mystereez uv=====
======= langwages   n wher th bodeez lay   ################
######################### n eye still love going 2 sleep
at nite ===== dreems uv my lovr in my hed   boing boing boing
zonk out=== boing boing boing zonk out zonk out zonk out

```
++++++++++++++++++++++++++++++++++++++++++++++++++++++++++++++++
++++++++++++++++++++++++++++++++++++++++++++++++++++++++++++++++
++++++++++++++++++++++++++++++++++++++++++++++++++++++++++++++++
++++++++++++++++++++++++++++++++++++++++++++++++++++++++++++++++
++++++++++++++++++++ +++    +++++++++++++++++++++++    +++++++++
+++++++++++++++++++++++++++   ++++++++++++++++++++++++  +++++++
++++++++++++++++++++++         ++++++++++++++++         ++++++++
+++++++++++++++++++++++++++++++++++++++++++++++++++++++++++++++
000000000000000000000000000000000000000000000000000000000000000
00000000000000000000000000000000000000000000000000000000000000000
##############################################################
```

how i feel abt my nu mind or brain

is just fine reelee ths may b th 3rd or
    4th wun 4 me in ths life that ium
    aware uv yes i can feel th previous
mind brain crumbuling n th othr mor
precise sharpr n yet way mor accepting
    roomier wun is kickin in or not
its what peopul sew oftn talk abt i think
whn they say theyr moovin on i still nevr
reelee moov on i keep in touch 4evr not
    clinging tho its veree ideel n as th
    amount uv peopul i know grows i cud
spend all day on th phone just keepin
    in touch well thats not entirlee trew
    uv aneewun is it   sew ths nu mind

  a lot uv informaysyun held in th previous
mind is being refiled in th nu wun like
  changing librareez mid streem n undr ground
    shelvs passing in th nite   what dew yu
        think anee uv ths is a pees uv cake it
    duz take patiens sum uv th time bcoz nu
        foldrs n nu filing systems windows on
th world well thats metaphor we gess at
what th mind brain cud b may b availabul
2 sew much mor thn we make room 4 allow

  fine our minds brains arint reelee compewtrs as
our minds brains change we adapt 2 nu scenes
n adopt nu insites 2 fit th shifting konstrukts what
we keep on giving 2 keep   going n what we take
pleez 2 love th journee what we can look eezilee
4give   2 b on our own road   with no fighting
    feel th majeek uv our bodeez n minds brains
    independent n growing furthr inside all th
    elements n th turning sun n moon rivrs uv

knowing n unknowing th soul heer 4 a whil
dansing independentlee uv its origins th

shine n gleem uv th mountin skin return 2
th elastik strings pull us back 2 no re turn
2 turning 2 th all wayze changing 4ward 2
no strings we cum from

sew ium going 2 enjoy ths nu mind each
day nite   all full uv surprizes evn mor thn th
previous wuns eye dont reelee recall in veree
precise detail tho i can if yu want its that a
lot wud b sew changd nd or lost in all th
transisyuns translaysyuns 2 th nu brain mind
ium now bcumming in

he lookd at me   ovr th fire lite n sd
yuv got a lot mor going 4 yu thn yu think

just thn anothr sky full shooting comet fell 2
erth liting his path ahed uv him   as he was
walking off   entring in 2 all th hi liting
darknesses n

me i was going back in2 th cabin 2 climb my
nite full uv stairs agen 2 th liquid n
soft grayzing stars

nothing is th whol storee

whatevr it is ium wanting

it cums if i dont need it 2cum
sew much   if i dont focus
          on th goal 2 much
     eye can live in th present
wher evreething is   can b
     th goals themselvs ar
       alredee fulfilling   if
          iuv plantid th seeds

eye dont know abt that part
totalee   2 tell yu th trewth
     its way 2 wet 2day 4 knowing
n anee proposisyun is put 2
          linear splicing testing
     dissekting   how manee in
          stances wud ths premis not
       apply 2 figurs apeer n disapeer
       sidewayze   n flickring in ths
       wet mirage   requests presences
sumtimes miraculouslee touching
       as whn we each   foolishlee
          wait 4 th wun oftn wiselee

we cant know   set up th tablow
          iul prepare th mirakul
       taybul

               peopul dont bcum mor
          lush tho they may with ths
               tropikul wetness plants dew
     flowrs hanging out sew far   in
               th moistyur what knowledg can
          apply 2 th suddn quaking uv th erth

th tektonik plates undr our
slippree vein filld feet   hmmmmm

ahhh or othr times tho
its all inkrediblee interesting

n takes our
breth away

writtn with george rigo n arlene lampert

ths is an in 2 print pome   imprinting

an in2 print kind uv pome an in2print porme an
imp printing rinting rintin 6 g im mi me ths is an
in2printing pomme de terr lushyus mc th em see 4 th
evning was is an in2print kind hoow veree uv yu mp
mp pm rin rin nir t t t t t t t t ttr tr na na na ma da
me em op op op po trin pim see si si shhhh o a
hhhhhhhhhhhhhhhh t t stimprin pome mwmw wm
.. po erm op me op   pomeeeeeeeeeeeeeeeee
yes ths is an in2 point po op print pome printing
imprimatuurya with yu now won own non nown
owwwwwwwwwwww na na an ana woan wwwn
imprintatuuraa ommmmmmmmmmmmmmmmmm
        moep om pe pe opem meop
it was whn he enterd th store late that nite thru th
gaybuld awning   thru   th kreekee door he sAw th
bodeez uv his frends splayd out on th countrs n
asparagus among th   produce n tinnd guds or gods
he wonderd whethr they wer ded or as his frend sd
onlee shopping   n he sd 2 his companyunn who was
kind uv jittree what he had herd from his frend that it
is possibul 2 sit still n still   travl no obstakul 2
breething   being sept in th mind we dew almost
evreething with   at th 5th wheel truck stop 7 timez
.. waaoooooaoaoaa aaaaahh omep popo mopo
       mope   po om epom
th vestibule in th willow shakee shakeea in2printing
imp rintin dendrite hippocampi corridora eskalatoraa
going down th up streem away filing filling rescue th
tremoring soul prsonn aliteez pome alitee ting ling th
ventilating hopes n murmuring allegianses ium with
yu ium alwayze with yu tum bul dry 4 me cud we
spin 4 each othr th plane was taking off n m m
memoreez uv tantalizing frustraysyun su preem sat
isfacksyuns o all th lovinng all th manee n various
kinds uv loving we dew with evreewun we respektfullee
can time is disapeering wher we can connekt

we ar all parts uv th same specees seach sew diff
rent n th same wer all breething whil we can let it
ourt th marmaduke n grangr chasm th lung fill uv
sound loving n whispring infinit versyuns uv th
storee zzzzz signing mi ma da sewla see saw see
see sighing love th touch th sky clouds erthn jelleez
th fire inside us   laffing 4 th road   a lovlee take off
               n soar   returning 2 our bodeez
evree wun jumpd up n skreemd at us DUCK eye
lookd around from my plkace on th floor as thos
bullets wer sparteeing n spraying th freshlee
scrubbd tiliks n linolessa   why duck i thot
. malard or ringworm kumquat   spiralling herons
lifting out uv ths messa we all rushd tord each othr
laffing n touching whoevr we ar ths is poma oma p
in2print imping   tin ar aviaaaa ravia   pommaa
radio laskee avyuraa   laskeeavyurnaa o pom
ma da pomma pomma omma ommmaa p
      waaaaaaaaaaaaaaaaaaaaaaaaaaaaaaaaaaaaaaay
               stimprin   moep
n if i feel sew sankshuaree   n fairlee zerox ths un
twin twining uv finding n letting burrows th down
loading   n in2printing mop appul pomma teer
glayshul duchessa n curtins ovr our eyez
n mor th imprinting out th rinting r othr theoret
ikaaaaaaaaaaaaaaaaaaaaaaaaaaaaaaaaaaaa
ravens ar largr n mor sleekee thn crows mattr finish
n smallr th raven sleekeeness almost runs uv purpul
bluish in th black in th changing lite n what did yu
say no b4 that o fine we did that alredee okay
xcellent   ping th joyousness sunset pang streeking
th hills pod uv killr whales jumping dansing sew hi
in th purpul marovian green blu watrs xcellent evree
wun uplifting th pome uv all uv us n each is us
issew in 2 printing prin ting imp lore ot
wher it grey mattr is sallow fervid tuck
endorfiniaaaaa lava lick lassting innnn

wher th brainbow blessings ar th lettrs in th images
th pickshurs in th lettrs words n woods uv tree allo
kaysyun merkuree dun zarreeo th pastel rivulets
algae moss silvr birch hes calling me ium kalling
him whn i pul th oods w 2 papier wil it releesing
konnekting ora spilling out uv each othr enraprt

  yur th holding barrell uv wings enkapsulating th
details   etching in th sub lingua mirroring times
  uv grace n lava aval laval valal lalva lalva ava vaaa
laaaa avvvv all 2 touch yu agen our minds tasting
sharing is all claptyura shouldr arms inside yu
inside me n letting b until jusqua nous parlons en
  core puis substans astro nomikul being sh
    ar ing each ama moa me omep mo em

  othrs lettrs modaliteez organizaysyuns uv lettrs
thots yu being in our bodeez *verasitee*   n tumult
laying with him   vera sitee looking ovr th lowr
mainland th port authoritee th ancient thames th
sparkling n sumtimes sinistr seine   always tho
languid he sighd n th sitee   time is timeless n nevr
apeerinng time is a word add a ton uv words is th
behaviour changing emblem ware housing n whn
he touches me calls me ium ther

  n whn he cums in2 me   n whn i cum in2 him
   compatibul neurona   hanging th balustrade

lifts th words manse chez melodeez uv inform
aysyun chan
        son uv evreething whatevr each blu
breth n
    danse in green goldn being

fires in toronto

we wer all entranced at last
seeing david cronenbergs crash
totalee hot at th uptown   sew
beautiful if yu get in2 it   sew
baleteek th pathos uv th self
destruktiv modes th carnage

n dusint evreething
crunch us all down th
technolojee is it liberating
us or crushing us our bodee
parts slammd by auto parts
squeezing us we selekt our
posyuns me i know we all have
self destruktiv enerjeez n self
konstruktiv we look 4 balansing
thees a lot uv us or playing with
onlee th self konstruktiv sides
letting th othr damaging go etsetera
th resolute auto eroticism   uhhh

heer thees peopul not sew torn
speshulizing crashing in2 neer
deth sequences manee timez until
thers no mor time eye found ths
film veree mooving iuv had a lot
uv sex in cars last bastion uv privasee
away from home fires interrupti
sew i was reelee looking 4ward 2 ths
wun n i love david cronenberg we all
crash soonr or latr   why put it off
thees peopul wer pursuing wun
bone brek at a time we have nu
metaphors nu terminolojee 4 th
processes

dusint say we undrstand it anee
bettr our needs 4 plesyurs pains
we take n what if what thees charaktrs
serch out is not what ium in2 duz not make
thees storeez in ths liquid flashing film
less convinsing hello evreewuns life
is not th same dew eye want 2 see mooveez
onlee abt peopul like myself   thees peopul
in crash theyr bodeez draped around each
othr n th beautiful car parts close ups uv
chrome close ups uv bodee parts james
spader sew amayzing   we ar all in ths
audiens sew hot with all ths n thn fire
alarms soundid bhind us veree loud we
wer alredee 2 hot 2 moov n thn thees fire
peopul with axes hoses n hatchets in
full fire regalia went raging down th far
rite side aisle rageing th moovee was
still on we wer all enrapturd veree hot
veree entransed seemd veree trew abt sum
things manee things we all went on gobbuling
th hot n rhapsodeek images sew brillyant n
totalee satisfying mesmerizing nothing wud
seem 2 deter us from n thn thees ushers
raged in n skreemd at us ar yu stupid cant
yu tell thers a fire get out we kept watching
sew caut up in th cinematographee sew
brillyant evokativ thn th film was shut
down n thn we reluktantlee left th theatr 2
hovr round th box offis 4 mor word on whn
we cud get back inside wher james spader n
holly huntr n elias koteas n deborah unger
 wer   n us

moths round ths fire sum in long coats men
women hovring waiting on th sign 2 get
back in it came xcellent we wer glued 2
th big skreen th intimasee n thn th fire

alarms agen fire peopul kompleet kostume yello
rubbr sumthing coats big yello metal hats kind uv
conikul carreeing axes hatchets hoses yu know
th far rite aisle n out th xit door n thn th ushers
yelling at us ar yu stupid they skreem at us th
fire has startid agen ium reelee feeling th word
stupid is veree pejorativ they pull th film oh
alrite weul go ths time they give us passess
ium ther th next day asking is th theatr still
on fire no th xcellent prson in th box offis sd
great eye sd n raged in wheww ther wer a lot
less viewrs hmmm i thot wer they shy 2 return
sew quik i wunt tell yu th

storee its sew beautiful sew much feeling
with thees devoteez wer looking in on theyr
most private lives parts uv wch bcum brokn
n transcendent in th manee inspiring close ups
also uv chrome n lethr seets human eyes thru
shatterd windshields car eyez have yu seen
christine th liquid yu can touch filming each
frame composisyun sew brillyant diagonals
steel glass lethr privaseez we ar all oftn caut in
th othr animals th othr cages we ar sew vulnr
abul alienatid from th majeek streem promise
who reelee gets 2 th serches 4 non xistens as
being hurts sew much oftn in ths physikul di
mensyun th allure uv th accidents uv   th
desires 4 evn tho i spend most uv my life trying
2 avoid pain n have nevrthless bin trappd in2
th claws uv sum othrs minds havint yu my
heart went out 2 thees brokn peopul coverd in
bodee casts n trauma   metaphora

how much mor suffring we oftn xperiens trying
2 avoid pain   yu know whn yu wake up with
an old wound bothring yu still scar tissu ther
that will nevr b remoovd   how can yu trust

molekular fabreek uv th magreetvia islands
n centraling offloading bringing in each dang
ling partisipul in a rave   aveh avaaa

uv kours with th east coast   th reelee east coast
langwage is used in diffrent wayze   thn in othr regyuns n
represents diffrent konstrukts   diffrent undrstandings
langwage is kultur n in like wise each regyunal
geographee delvs in makes its own   intrpretaysyuns
jestyurs invensyuns realiteez ahhh   realiteez
thers a kontravershul kontra   puntal   reflexif
innovativ   2 th point wher john   uv th lumbargo   red
pine fethrs spredding th   length uv his bodee wch oftn
he tuckd neetlee in b tween his shouldrs   n o th moon
was rooling n roll   ing ovr thos purpuling hills redolent
with mauv   streeks n calcium red chromia tendrilling
all thru th   lowr plateaus baked red klay hundrids uv
deep holes peckd out swallows live nest in   side fly out
from   balkoneez hi on ths bird condo   cliff   undrside
n th pastyurs filld with cows n sum bulls   n crows in th
treez like notes in a bar dots n   shadows in th
spaces btween leevs braches un   mooving n thn
swirling off n at th bottom land   neer th lake shore
marshes beevrs work ripping n build   n eaguls   sevn or
eight uv   them 2gethr wizend lofting push up soar
n glide a gud sign in multipul canada gees returning not
honking heds necks lungs silent   wings mooving up n
down flapping on th air ium listning 2   sounds drums
keeping them aloft n flying   th gees ar   drumming
parts uv our mewsik cum from birds wings   drumming
2 fly 2 stay up each word he sd is also diffrentlee placed
thn pushing 2 get up mor   n rising in th breef vacuum
keeping 2 fly   th relaysyunships btween   praktikul
divine   spiritual n romanteek n health ishews   divine n
carnal   r th same eye sd   how all that informs   veree
diffrentlee thn sum wher els   in th stretching huge
geographeez wher we all find ourselvs rivrs lakes oceans
mountains plains in an infinit   colleksyun   uv lang
wages   cumming   xpressing

sum protektid   sins they ar not alredee with ipso
fakto use cumming 2gethr   we ar each othrs
geographeez   a bilingual countree with 2 n 3 nd
manee naysyuns simultaneouslee 2 b n share n b
ourselvs b4 n as textualizing now th worlds largest
countree in taking care uv th land places each othr
wher we all find ourselvs inkluding evreewun with in
relees from   th inkrediblee   debilitating hierarkikul
kontests nowun remembrs th reesons 4 aneemor
going thru them a necessaree phase 2not needing
them did they we   evr know th terribul hurting ovr
reakting damaging reveng arketypal dramas   dont
they totalee suck bcum ar un interesting what a
waste uv time   whatevr yu figur reinkarnaysyun
such a short time heer or not   wher is heer n th
dimensyunal   transisyunalizing whethr a dreem
pipe dreem wish list 4 immortalitee

    from a lettr 2 a lovd wun n ourselvs *ar yu   bittr*
that yu mite not b immortal   n decide 2 make reems uv
troubul 4 evreewun who loves yu yr   reveng trip will
sumday no longr engross yu   reveng 4 what who can stop
th cycul uv violens let it go look in2 yr own heart yu
havint alwayze playd fair have disembled th plot was 2
    thik 2 redee disguising yr non involv
    ment slipping out th side 4est let
    ting them fight it out thn radio
    ing in soothments 4 them 2
   declare clovr n dignia remembr yr loving
  ovr all leefee burgundee n signia uv
 loving our diffrenses n loving our same
 nesses protekting both and sins th violens
is from made up konstruktid inventid from irrekon
silabul konstrukts abstrakt noun xklusyuns that dont
xist why not get off it sylabul sylabi syblantheen th
lacquerd laminating hot lava flow find th spot ohhhh
who can call yu just give love compassyun what els can
yu dew its terribul 2 b fritend uv sum wun yu love
  espeshulee if they cant help it th
   damage they dew

life   may b   apokriful

yu wait n wait 4 his call is it an ice kreem or is it
  a wall   a nippul a wave   a save   sum rippul

                         or a touch uv gold glistn in th
     moonlit shade changing as th moon n erth turn
     tord sparkling darkness   from th previous lites

yu remembr th voyage we tuk in th land uv snow
     icikuls gatherd sumtimes 2 close around our
                                 hearts n
  th monkeez uv our minds playd 2 hard sumtimez
  against ourselvs n th remindrs wud flow inside th
  tentakuld harbor way b4 th glacier wud start melt
                                    ing

     whats th importans we thot a littul erlee spring
                     adventyur   th card *procrastinate*
     came up   n we pushd on thru th huge blocks
        spires uv ice veree filld n chopee seez it was
     reelee 2 erlee in th tidal turns th astronomee n
     klimate 2 ventyur ths far out in 2 th various n
                             moodee oceans

     we saw walruses jumping on unstaybul ice sheets
     huge see lions glowring restless intro spektiv
     pacing n looking 4 chomping studeeing th aqua
     mareen green watr 4 fishes who wud want 2 go
        undr with them b that wet   thundr lightning
     ice cracking thn shifting continuing silens creek
                     ing   th breth uv th world

     dew yu remembr us tipping our way thru th ice
           kastuls floating sew deep almost 2 th bottom
     spikes shooting out from anee moment we cud

92

split opn our watree path n th times we layd 2
gethr aftr cumming whn bells wud sound in yr
hed n yu wud go back up on yr watch

iuv sumtimez talkd uv ths with frends   that we cud
nevr go out 2gethr   tho eye wud have n why wud
that have bin a destroyr 2 yu   uv our majeek timez our
getting it on seklusyuns

it was anothr long wintr th ice slow 2 melt   i dont evr
know whats going on   2 happn next with peopul
or life chill listn 2 th sound uv woolvs in th nite wer
heer now on ths erth   pleysyurs surround us eye
wonderd why did yu take sew long i want 2 put it on
yu   th feelings eye had pennd up inside my summr
                                 heart   konstraind
with sew much waiting time isolate lerning   howevr
faltringlee   2 put th focus on myself   eye found ths

ice world vizualee sew beautiful entransing th molekular
tensyun uv ths glayzing world tho i knew it cud crack
           n hurl us down   like yu sd wun time it isint
           fair 2 yu indikating me n eye thot whats fair
           frends ar dying horribul deths they sum
           timez find theyr pees with n peopul we love
      byond imagining leev us we konfined by kontext
arint availabul 2 othrs we hurt by not being with them
we spend 2 much time alone 2 digest n let go big moans
      why digest thn go out dansing get our soul n bodee
2gethr 4 us 4 me in2 th mewsik

ths is reliabul getting it on i dont think i want anee
mor   *eithr* etsetera n othr skripts storeez mooveez as
if eye wer a charaktr in a scene life full time can b 2
           much sorrow   attachment let go get in
      2 th dansing n thn waiting 4 yu 2 call   walking

93

ovr an ice field 2 get back home   snow falling
thru th skeleton treez draped in ice lyrikul brave
n th ground undr hard   n may b shuddring

it was a green island we made it 2 washd ashore on
th translucent n hot beech creashurs uv morsels
    succulent n digestibul hung from thees tropikul
treez oranges as well appuls bananas   we made
rice fields   n at nite   th winds wud cry   howl uv
delishyus pleysyurs tastes n strange sub equatorial
    feers sparks from th fire roasting cobblr fish
                hypnotizd us

    what is th ironee th twist uv fate plot device
    wayze in 2   th art making abt th self esteem
weemsbee remembr him   wrote in his diaree th
sew long dayze n nites giant panda fish falling from
ice clouds   or was th world just turnd upside down

ther wer spirits in th winds i wud listn 2 no longr
hauntid by what cud b clouds fingring th air as in
no longr wanting reelee 2 moov 2 find yu bcum
doubtr reclews th yu shifting be leef seeing is it
anee storee   n beleev agen as i dew find n agen yr
in evn with all my sumtimes cawsyun n inward
ness   in th voyage

    eye moov my hed btween yr legs   find agen

                    sum temporaree home

ice storm 98

ium watching cnn ctv cbc 4
dayze kebek its treez destroyd
by th hevee ice most uv th powr
lines down lites out lives in
th dark day aftr day th cold

deepens weeks ium surfing
cnn shows a street in montréal
i know wher sum xcellent frends
live th camera prowls th snow
n ice coverd street THERS THEYR
HOUS UNDR ALL TH SNOW ICE
N FALLN TREEZ sew much
dangr n th air cracking

i think th camera now approaching
my frends porch will ring theyr bell
n i can see whethr theyr okay n fine
or will they cum out n wave n say
hi bill wer xcellent dont worree

THS DUZ NOT HAPPN N IT IS THEYR
HOUS i dont see them aneewher ium
disapointid stunnd n wuns agen eye
realize tho i will 4get that teevee is
not reelee as intraktiv as i think its
not evn virtual

ium veree close 2 th skreen my eyez
up in2 th glass i can see theyr not
home   a week latr we talk i find
out they stayd at parents place it
was not eezee ther   n manee uv th

beautiful treez on theyr street ar
rippd apart ded from th brutal
cold n ice

why isint ther mor time

                    2 speek is yr mouth gettin 2 dry o silvr
saliva me soon bathing th kaktus uv th pricklee
embryo moistening th message lubrikating th lion
        why isint ther mor time 2 dreem   seems
evree time a doktor eemsbee mastrs th climax n th
4play is lengthening dunes ob sarrows satrdayze n
 lost tissu th personnel changes fine
                                        why isint ther
mor time 2 fuck   yes eye had a great dreem last
nite evreething kost half as much as it duz now n
we ar all erning twice as much as we dew now ths
way our chances bon chance uv breking evn wer
evn greatr mor secure mor shur mor sertin allur
th hmmmm

why isint ther mor time 2 love we can 4give wev
bin hurt n bcum waree uv othrs n admit wev hurt
as well our serch 4 mistr ms rite narrows with time
n xperiens yet our boldness nevr faltrs   yes we 4get
its onlee love that saves us n work that also uses
our kapabiliteez we feel wasint it kalld reel enhansd
kore happening k k k k k ore ora gonn   ahhh
whn mistr ms rite is always inside us hmmmm
ahhh
        why isint ther mor time 4   dansing we need 2
make that   nowun can dew it 4 us   oh

mor time 4 romansing same list prhaps why isint
ther an island   mor time
 uv lost tissus   why isint ther mor time
     why isint ther mor time 4 WHAT

we kum 2 yu on a rathr pink n replex blu nite on th
northern shores uv planet love   planet love PLANET
                    L O V E whil its trew
th depleesyun in th O zone now covrs th antarteek
as i dont need dominating peopul in my life he sd..

i didint know they wer dominating aneemor they can b
kum sweetr in retrospekt   longs i dont see them 2 oftn
i gess maybe sertinlee ium not insecure   th way i usd 2
he sd flicking his ash sd whatevr his eyez opning eye lovd
them n th beautee uv his sinceritee in th candul lites
b fine ths is xcellent big time   rovr n ther was ths
bed n that bed n leeving in th morning he sd sighd
                    n leeving in th aftrnoon
                        n leeving in th evning what
els evreewun back 2 work   puttin my pants back on
i get pattid go 4 a piss n leev
get sum split
direktlee aftr
swetr in retro
build a towr 2gethr
  watch it

    n is it trew they whoevr lovr bills latr they didint
  reelee love us how cud they live with us 4 sew
    long othr sew we hung out 2gethr living with ths
  qwestyun giving ourselvs comfort that way n hungr
                        in our hands

why isint ther mor time   2   breeth   2 b o piddul
  th valleez get a grip n tangereen lafting sarios th
  tangoed n treelined plentee opines   th windows n
  doors n
                ths is 2day   yes send a massage b a
                            message uv
                    endless words n beds uv
                  pepprmint flesh   smells n musk
                ths is a pickshur uv me in my apartment
          in toronto its a subway car green toxik
              fumez   iuv drank invisibul ink   sew yu
          cant see me ium ther tho smiling in th
        green violent tint n hayze n waving at yu

      hey wait a minit ium 4getting abt yu thees
    hot smells ar cumming in 2 me   ium 4getting th
      major theems heer   rippuling animal
                            flesh scents husk
        a strangr wun apeers

                            97

time n space ar sew intrmixd   is it seemless th what is
    o god   at last   hands on my   ness ar
    tits n cock   n mouth me
we live in th big tent   mouth me   this is
  uv big time   our   touth me   lot bettr thn
  own time like th   mouth me   sum fals
  buttr fly   bettr thn   mouth me   accusaysyun
    worree ovr ee   mouth yu   me
    zeee   zed   o mouth   me   or hold on 2
or me orm   yu south me   like a life
  saying stay   bouth yu me   preservr im
  can yu   outh me   ploord pleez
shift geers n go   douth yu me   dont go ium
orm dorm lorm   fouth yu me   all th lites in
was it us all   gouth yu me   all our eyez
bettr thn sorree   houth yu me   that was th
  individual being   routh yu me   best thanks
    tunnuls uv fate   uv his pomes   man thanks
  along th rivr uv   end in kriteria   as gatheerd a
    rathr submergd   citee all our   wings n tails
  gesturing rage   in th cumbrland   chambrs
    late on time   me louth me   outh me
    cumming up   vouth yu me   not robotik
  4 air breeth in   wouth yu me   not programmd
  n down start   zouth yu me   responses
    th n agen   zouth me
    keep going   zouth yu me   spirits rushing by
              zouth yu me   rapid transit
onnnnn   zouth yu me   nimbul cum u lay
  onnnnnnnnn   zouth yu me   syuns bettr
onnnnnnnnnn   zouth yu me   thn   slandr
  onnnnnnnnn   zouth zouth   o lee ander
at wits end   zouth   zouth   th littul town uv
  if time stops   zouth   zouth   wher ar
  wer not   mouth   mouth   we if time
  heer   mouth   mouth   disapeers
  singing   mouth   me   mouth   from ths
  molecules   mouth   yu   mouth   dimensyun
  mouth   mouth   mouth   wer in sum
at oms   mouth   mouth   othr wher

th breth heart uv th world

a trip 2 th moon

4 george méliès *le voyage dans*
la lune 1904

avant lunaseez th carp ay suave th tango notre vies
s'illumine   a court sequens   not curt sequins shining
celebrate   celebrate lookit th diagram it can b dun
a veree discursiv metaphysikul scientifik scene   th
implikaysyuns

dansing girls 1 2 3 4   how manee   rockits goin off

its a great rockit space ship   wowww a trip 2 th moon

th face in th moon sew smiling antisipating   we land
owwwwwww   a stye in th eye   that hurts

ths is not on gossamer wings   o no 2 much xhaust

we ar n ar not erthlings   dpending   moon landing
mannd   maned
mandling   o
moanding
jubilaysyun   evreewher

undr blankits stars comets tailing   evreething is
beautiful   g nite
bon nuit
g nite
sleep now   pinealitee

rings around th   moon
wings ROUNd th   pillows
sings around th   carress yu

is that snow   or galakteek sequins   is ther food heer
whers th bathrooms   thees moon vegetaybuls ar
trewlee
HUGE

thees moonshrums we can see them grow n GROW

A MOON CREESHUR BOUNCES OUT n happilee
    greets erthlings manee mor moon creeshurs
        anothr court moon courtlings xcellent raging
moon creeshurs ar veree akrobateek erthlings dont like
them moonlings ar in much bettr shape erth lings hit
                                th moon creeshurs

moon creeeshurs can disapeer in suddn smoke dont yu
wish yu cud sumtimes   erthlings ar bad 2 moonlings
    moonlings xpell th erthlings from theyr moon home

 ahh back 2 erth its a bust on th moon cudint make it
ther

 war n nostalgia twin foez uv serenitee   huh deep

 erth is prettee nice 4 a whil yet   a lovlee harbor can b
resting places   from all our lives   th moon   hmmmm
  wev bin ther they say   eye wundr can erthlings get
    bettr   ths harbor   a prfekt composisyun setting n
  2morro who knoes   PARIS awards medals selebrate
                                sellabrate
        sleep now   agen   we werent gone long

        dansing in th lullabye moon dreems   humming
  our lunar melodeez hunee thank yu luna lulla LUNA
bye seez una al lull   luna lullaluna seez una el 1 lab

a la   1 lee a luna lulla lallu a luna seeeee lulla lobi
luna   leela dont tell me aneething linear pleez thers bilo

    thers lobee hi bi   how ar yu long time no seez
no wun breething fire door down yr neck keep breething
            yulla ullaaluuuu

    lulla luaa ul la lulla lulla la lee olulo olulooooaa
leeeaauu
laluu lalee le lalul leela naauul una la uuna laa uhh
  luna leela luna leela o la o leeleeaa laaaaa leeeeeeeee
luuuuaaaaaaaaaaaaaaaaaaaaaaaaaaaaaaaaaaaaaaaaaaaaaaluuu

101

pavlovs dog 1

wud yu rathr onlee b
ths happee thn fullee
trusting agen n gettin
whackd whappd wun
mor time as yu cirkul th
reel prize yr own focus
on yrself   innr serenitee
yr love happee being
without goal attainment
alredee is not self having

bells ar ringing great smells
b careful   sumthing mite
not work having can b valu
 n thers no food nun not
dont care abt things yu have
 no powr ovr agen n get reelee

miserabul   sew thers a ringing
sum wundrful perfumeree from
th larkspur hydrangea roses n
plums pears n a kleer lake neer
by valu can protekt its virtual
realitee sumwun may honor
theyr agreement with yu if they
dont sum thing els may still
cum up gud

happeeness is sew tempting yu
dont want 2 fall apart if yu dont
get it   meditating tails or heds
oftn its not binaree its in th 7th
or third opsyun th magik resides
wait 4 it hungree awkward re
wired agilitee taking yr time
fr sure but redee 2 leep

tracks uv moistyur   on th

b a r r i n g t o n

sqweemish was yelling agen   if ium going 2 end
up ths weird feeling   n th lightning fingrs sew
skrapeing   intruding gouging in2 my hed ovel n
waladee   sir salad carree th wastel out in2 th
red hedg hog   tormentine west uv th estern
alliagate   esteem was phoning th room at last
warm n shifting indoors th eye bleetid n scabrous
th lid
a z u r a
buttons look liked taped ovr th
kreesd slit wher th prson sew far deep inside lay
veree much so cawshus byond redeeming turidfrm
tanning his own motivs   n being sew hard on him
self drying ovr his heart on kaktus it was not like
working on par advize saw who spreding my will in2
th far cornrs uv th tomb 4get will eye sd
n th dialektik didint
it 4get us sew i kalld th room wanting 2 b in love n off th
street in2 th chesterfield n boldend forth legs getting less
shakwaa eee as th kaffeen kikd in life goez on she sd
well eye hope sew i sd o he sighd arint we all th fall guys
4 a bunch uv powr freeks pushing us a round smacking
us heer ribbing us ther koff up bones til we feel th in
adekwasee they want us 2 well protekt yrself eye sd
sum peopul yu will love in yr life lives will b meen
spirit whn th unluckee trend is taking a brek lookup
n notis fr sure they kant ovrwhelm yu n that wunt
tire yu noth ths life biz is less thn a picknick fr sure
prettee tatterd th homilee tablo on th selfdestrukting
walls th papr n th joists sew fraught interior pillows
fucking uuuh uuuuh goin all th way inside th
current connektor boldlee goin thru all th moist
squish tomaotoez n peechus what we will sail seew
far 4 if we can find anothr agen encore tho entirlee
tongues n lava b happee 4 yr devosyun th mauv
sunsets pink brite streemrs across th sky

blayzing trails 4 midnite riders they cum heer 2 find theyr
passyun its reelee not availabul 2 them inothr parts uv th
societee howevr benign theyr not going 2go thru th bull
shit aneemor th passing or deferring rock skreeming
kleening lingrs a long shot uv that field gold n tawnee
silkee passing thru my hed as eye washd up aftrwords
n milkee greeting klassik as if ther isint aneething 2 put
out sum uv us wer just 2 uprite was it th visor killing us
aneeway or passing out in th northern hills nova skosyan
accent sumtimes cumming back whn ium ther lav arlee
waverlee th inkubaysyun period sew long now who knew
whn life cud b still uplifting thru evn all th suddn greeving
zarons gurp grap guba o fossils n endless green my hearts
breking he sd dont get sew hung on him eye whisperd
saverlee see breez see windo an arm sighing a long th
pane th candee grass glass ships sew ghostlee savoring
choppeeness cummin in 2 shore rushin out now sum
wun wave sout a sliding door wave back sum guys wall
king down 2 th swimmin hole in theyr town speeding up
chois uv kon strukts away is great vishyun tunnul waning
moon he droppd in sd heud had 12 operay syuns in th
last three weeks n was still determind 2 rage touch ther
n ther he was zarons turn th watr onn fossils n endless
green no murdr on its mind eye card 2 tell th ownr n he
sd peopul n his frend with such dansing eyez kept say
ing 2 me i know wev met b4 yeers yes eye sd getting a bit
hard n what was 4 me 2 lifetimes ago it was great we wer
sailors 2gethr on ths great ship nowun evr stoppd fuck

ing alla time zaneen rafftlers n sew loving n loyal it was
xcellent he sd n th sailing adventyurs wer th veree best
its all 4 fun slash dot margareen pick a peek a sorrow
oddo cook ee dew yu want 2 b like happee they get upset
bcoz th sound uv th birds isint just rite 4 them they eye
brow th musturd hills being coverd with snow n huge dust
part ikuls still i stayd assertif therud bin no clah kaybor
or mirror intangenshul calm mageabul self eye was ovr th
falls now n we wer awardid 4 falling thru th weekend ceil
ing uv th stormaway hostelree onto th guys in th bed be
low it was historeek punkshul all laffing 4 dayse thn sly
lee tucking it away in yes well he met sum wun els but sd

he nevr undrstood why i stoppd cumming around
rafftrs uv celllulous   TREETEEZ
                DOLPHINS   moistyur kissing each
othr cumming up 4 air his hands arms asround my
breething soul i was gone   lojeeko sero bello a all
looking for
                all looking for
                ll looking   or
                a l oo ink   ro
                la   kooig   rof
th endless shore uv th oval th fleetingness evree
things ar embossing with as th ocean always raging
n brekrs pound sew neerbye evreewher th cruekteez
n th wistid   th typhoon typhrous o my i thot merg
ing with yu how i love yu how i love yu   what dew
we know n   th laffing in th musturd egg or 2 eye
sd packing sum mor hay in2 th bins th horses crim
son red stalyun swetee aftr th mid nite ride all th
green lush snapping back dragonA N SIGHING HE
IS TH PRSON 4 ME HIS EYEZ N BRAIN OPN LIKE
NEVR B 4   WEEREE UV WAREE FOLDING OVR
NEUROLOGIA UP CUM LET ME TOUCH LET MY
FINGRS LINGRSONG giant poanda fish nowun evr
stoppd fucking on ths boat he addid us on deck brin
ging singing th salt air breething   laffing n chorus
sing til our lungs wud burst like as not up n look
ing in th morning two pairs uv hands running ovr
my bodee in my ham mock sew fine koffee aftr ths
hmmm i sit n listn 2 th konsert from paris mewsik
like jacques ibert bit prokofiev scenik narratifs haun
ting passages ium sitting   undr th full moon in th
karibu heart ache replaying th fine voyages eifeel
towr sirens artists n dansrs running tord each othr
symbols almost brek th reseevr th great cedar tree
holds me in time n space i cud eezilee waft out from
it was reelee th height uv th ski lift not neer anee
harshness   we wer siting around trying 2 tame sum
book worms they wer jumping highr n highr n th
wistids sew trechrous 2 bad e minus

mix
intensyuns n   pett
strange ro ads n car   ing   all th runik sund
  plentee   storee a mergr reno
    ta
wishes   stone   change   program   change th
instruk   syuns   wizards   releef   heightend   a
lapsword   reekr   favora   tim   time   love
south 4   th boats   inn travelling   thru   horizon
rumords   2 b   glayzing   hi   with th   parts
uv th   vehikuls   abandoning   th detour signs
cum   in 4   th   nodding   with th   admixtyur
uv del   monteyz   creem style   corn n th pick
up th   majeek sye   th stones we   came 4   didint
yu d tour   wings   n mufful   patterning   snow
feet th glass song   withruers   how eye lovd him
his lip   looking   in2   mine hooking   taking me yes
whn we   kissd that   was thn nostalgia   4 politikul
or prsonbal   replikaysyuns4   what nevr was   well
that was   n moov on   aneeway   a stirring   in th
  telephone timor   waitid   batch uv   hatching   kall
th living streeming poles   sandal wood   bleeching
agen b travelling thru th horisoz   announsments n
what   yu sd n th   emerald monkeez   sleeping
in th moist   purpul gardn   vista blu hemlock seems
  n mauv humming   birds silentlee fly around them
gessing at th composisyun   uv realitee life being n
flite patterning   wings a mufful glayzeeong n gladning
in2 th aspiring sacrumult alredee heer   th tengibul
tangetishul wavers b   mouths larking   n th ystrday
2day glade song heer is wher we ar   dew yu like heer
th sumpuositeez   returning th wire msplaced
vachons replaysing th zenifiter via marginal   sankteers
goomp poomg g   m g ium back in hell agen he sd
but its   gud 4 my writing   sew thn ther   was a
raging t word toronto tornado tee timid tenors
suddnlee   gallopping
enraptyur theyr desire full uv wanting n   decisyun as if
that cud change anee outcum n   n   de flax
abul   th wavering sound uv   oo   rn
harold   hebrides   ph   ve
  ka ka milyun times thirtee   ty   ta

106

whn wud it stop all ths dying opn n green windos
insted they say going 2 goldn scarlet   cobalt blu
shining perl starecases envelopd in yelo white lite
flooding th konschusness with   grateful being it
cud b all th disapointments th danse moovs on b
cum sew sad ovr   dependent on 4 mor miltaree takeovrs
thees ar th wuns its hard beng a kolonee   thers alwayze
an empire speek 2 him thru th monkee whispr th loving
nevr ends we can have it go on n on   n 2 all th lost wuns
isint that al uv us sumtimnes our deranged estimaysyuns
xpektaysyuns gryphons n roar roar un nameabul name
lesswuns suddnlee looming in2 th microscope xamining
th bananas leevs tendril vegetaybuls   o no not reech
ing agenm th crew moistend   th barrington n sew ful
sum sighing th great whales reechd ovr 2 shed teers its
hard enuff ths lofe without bcumming hard on wunself or
hard wunself alone 2 long th joints stiffn   tinkshur now
we can dew set that agen   wuns mor   ovr th floor bord
star whistul th mangrel   lick heer   huh squeez ther
sereena orga neekia whn we wer kissing i felt like ths is
all ium livea livuu livid th colors uv my innr eye balls th
tandorium a uv th low hanging   trellis in th rocking rivr
bed n up at five swab th decks n memoreez whn yu
crashd at three toll taking mirrar th longr socks n th
crossing allwayze uv that street n finalee   th snows
melting n whn we kiss its reelee all ium feeling why
is ther aneething els bcoz its interesting th refrains
n th activiteez uv th soul weeving   melting eyez
glimp pingul t th word restrain   o   ee   pins
discovr   zee go zeep reep th
         orange guba werent ther   alwayze n sew
       rushing evn th hard   parts   ar eezee whn
aftr th feeling eye grope thru ium not with yu o sir
galaxee wasint th see   murmuring 2 us telling us 2
keep on loving reegardless uv   th forms we take
bcum ar join in th unklaiming   nameless rocking
dansing th formaliteez as if   ther wub b ab
annosent state i wud write   pomes in th sand
gathr vegetay buls   undr th   sweltring bulbs n
beeno madam tremulous th wanting man breeth
                                                    deep

trikaptyur th musculs 2 b takn in by th great glayzd
   eye cumming in on th see bords cumming 4 us
   all we cud dew was 2 love each othr   th luckee
amount uv soon soon   sooooon weul reed ths
nuspaprions braveree tracing th lettrs inside th tree heer
eye am loookin at th karibu sky as th washes winds   pull
them off th line 4 they freez totalee ium trying2dew th best
i can he sd 2 his sistr in th sky its a fast tour n drop ping
sum yu love can b th   most cruel xpektaysyuns   deer
remembr i know okay   eye sd thanks let th vessel
 emptee pour dew fakts   bgin with theree me ovr n turn
me out whats ther ideas making limbs   witnesses ium
spilling moov portals petals not   reech th crew with th
rotting vegetaybuls we had 2 make dew   n th previous
announsd randoria in th rockin rivr bed time 4 th word
restrains th bow activiteez   uv th soul weeving melting
eyez byond dual isteek pandor let that   go james was
inkreesinglee bside him self n dansing with   suaysyun
susan in th onlee piano isimo pinaforte kaladaa stakkato
how manee lives aftr th feeling was not th see murmuring
2 tell us 2 keep on loving   not 2 fall 4 aneewuns war
games regardless uv th forms we take th formaliteez
as we walkd thru th hallowd gates uv ye olde tryin 2
get 2 taheetee a way from th skreeming n th religyus
pain deth kult   n th temperate sell out zones
repliikants uv th empire work ethika destroying our
lives wanting th bones 2 warm up   cult cud dissolv
well leev me out uv it   eye want 2 play b my self
work yes but not that   way etsetera lookin in2 th
crystal   streetcars saxaphone   barges traktor
banana bords uv our   minding limb tree novas
treenors is ar 4gottn   mothr didint say how manee
dayze therud b like ths dan sd well its ten minits n i
hope th pots not burning   in th stew that was sum
storm last nite seeing th pinksew agile deer dansing
in th threddee icikul stringee   enklosures apeering
re emerging 9 hours 2 b 4gottn 12 hours 2 go home
lost words arrows rocks splitting them selvs out uv
th waves n grounding wasil event shula keep trindul
leeprs tail recalls thru th nite surroundid by humm
ing wires mega volts resonating throb th redee weer

men n women   in uniform   mooving thru th forest
    shadows intent scouring   looking 4 us   not 2 pin
anee medals on   uv kours   its abuse uv powr   not
gendr anee way that   engendrs attributes   uv destruk
    syun n manipulaysyun   wer such shy winnrs   test
    ing on th stand on   patheteek fhallaseez n   anthro
pomorphisms apeering reapeering   WE WER DIGG
ING OUR WAY UNDR TH ROOTS UV TH GIANT TREEZ AS
FAST AS WE CUD NOT RELENTLESS UNIFORMS WITH
THEYR SKAPEGOATING   HATE IDEAZ FILLING THEYR
HEDS   NOT OUR PROBLEMA   9 hours 2 b parshulee
4gottn   yet lernd ths is what peopul ar capabul uv   7
hours 2 get on with it   n we still go on   anothr koffee
thru th train track window fukan daylite or what or eros
th murmuring hill us spain he sang as he lay dyin what
els we cudint make out   we wer sobbing sew   in thees
woods n th klustrs uv tangor   ovr th hill side   green eree
laffing gentlee vapora n lost words arrows rocks splitting
th grange dreem selvs   out uv th waves   trindl leeprs
isint it disapointing how littul our specees is evolving n is
endangring itself   tassul th crown n liddage n linden see
th sellular town   memoree   gaining on   th hottest
commangular or sending ths lettr   folding inside itselvs
yeh   eye cud hardlee moov in ths regyun   rain town th
mistr premier is   taking our food   th rulrs   dont care
whethr we eet as we bravelee rage on pendr n zeeplux in
th ardor   th yard spreding   giving   kissing fields sew
hollow inside we moovd in 2   th training areas laffing a
bit cum 4 lemon aid in de voon th land uv innr pees our
guns redee th lands uv inndr seedling   well my moppets
thers enuff tangereens 2 peel n fraktyls 2 gathr 4 th weep
ing is abundant drixxul politiks resebtr seeping in 2 i was
wrong 2 have a gud soak he sd bettr i had raunching first
whn i cud grab it dew yu recall   can yu th nite yu wer
sew kind 2 me sd 2 take care   it was a street kornr n th
winds erlee evning sew n th   stars n th moon sew hevilee
in our sharing gayze thru moralisms n garbage n killing
tortur territoreez nevr   undrstood n judging n
skapegoating wev all fukd up   pass th ball around now
wev lernd we want 2 b away   from th bullshit TH
                                                    LIST   uv

alone 2 long th joints can stiffn   is life pavlovan my how
she cud danse pharmasutikul kompaneez   in trest in
vakseens xcusing me n farrows in th   green est chairs
who wud b ther 2 carress them now ium sorree   my frend
or me flicking th ash in th direksyun uv nobodee arrivd n
trying dew yu remembr th nite yu wer   sew kind 2 me sd
take care uv myself yud nevr 4get me   driving off it was a
street cornr rhap sodee deepning mazurka heeting up n th
winds erlee evning so n th stars moon   hevilee in our
sharing gayze eye wantid 2 go sleep with yu immediatelee
n our destineez taking us evreewher els   n blah blah n i
see yu in th day time same thing   leeving chariot on lee
sew less intimaten ium gonna   say 2 yu n thees
formaliteez uv th day time heer in hell remembr its gud 4
th writing or sending th lettrs with   knoking xcuse me o
don get sew   dreeree   ium looking   4 th koffee cup
commandeering   dont doubt th wayze that brout u heer
my legs carree me thru he sd

if i werent writing ths iud go reelee crayzee   reelee un
happee ths can keep me going fr how long ar they mine its
anothrmayze i know anothr path tarrow   starring in
westrlee radiators cum socks pluggd in semiphors uv our
needling jellee sprites spitting out from th carpet reeches
2morro iul put out th cigarett n danse th present trying th
side uv th dock wharf n thrown   that n memoreez uv
passyun introdusd them selvs   why cudint he love me
whn i love him sew rid ing   with me thru th hurricane
th reinkarnativ wheedling talk   we cant eliminate th
needless suffring visiting a frend in   th hospital saltee
teers in my eyez abt data cumming in abt time n changing
place ask ing thn is ther reelee a place put   th eggs in
heer n scrambul ths teers reelee hurt soonr or   latr evree
thing n thn madness he sd or dew   we begin that way
anothr abstrakt noun konsept based on   dualitee ium
sew kleer at leest life dusint   make sens 2 us nowun
reelee knows huh know if ther isint greef thers no being
alive at th begining we love n receev love n make sure as
we can we ar being fed thn dot dot ths info my frend ferns
at th creek time aneewun

know what it is he sd start heer no n that she dusint
see him aneemor no he noddid we dont know what it is
life nowun duz me ium pretending ium happee sum
times he sd evn whn ium not yes he sd nodding n falling
asleep ium sorree ium nor keep yu awake i sd yu ar gud
companee he sighd running his arm around my shouldr n
his hand on my chest i herd th teevee yelling our our
private encountrs with th lord i thot uv th militaree indus
trial komplex private enkountrs with th lord th prson
ium in love with just got diagnosed positiv i love him sew
much feel eye dont deserv ths love   n n n cudint it
grow sumtimes ium not afrayd at all n we have sew
much fun th veree best thn th diagnosis n ium thinking
uv handling it n thn i realize how ium not handling it at
all we can th teevee went on sew thn graosimplo westen
leandron burrowing on th free fax mason ree uv terrified
briks agate sayze ovr th fr fr frosteee wayze th gardiner
xpress cars jumping   theyr rail ings sweep th parfume
igus tangludid thn they walkd out thn they walkd in we
toked in th raftrs in th off room secret almost door 2
sky stars cold hot smoke thn   back in n in side whats
reelee th church uv my chois   dansing with othr guys
rockin with or without coupling each making letting his
be ing rock 2 th nameless   god goddess uv 2gethr with
out text or xplain its also uv kours   manee othr events
but ths wun its sew great 4 me   thn she th leedr sd we
must keep thees peopul free by   making them poor we
can b rich n they can b poor evree wun has sumthing is
poor sumthing 2 have eye askd not reelee being grantid
an audiens yes they sd up th   regyuns uv narrowlee
missing th southpaw rain forest ing th cattul n th ballet
tites framing th upstanding burokrateek reespons playing
on th pacifika dont yu want 2   getaway in each
individual being rockin in th crush sinceriteen th lite
shined in our eyez agen   its not a deth sentens n eye
bgun talking with th othr men in th ward i found i cud
dew things 4 othrs in spite uv th insults   th flak intern
alizd how tuff it reelee gets not takn in by th had whiperd
with me   they had 4gottn had made me a bit dangrous
suddnlee in love getting past th voices find   myself
massaging my frends back n being useful n not ovrlee
cheerful or

studlee pimpul biy it wakes up stiff in th morning   4
getting my greef letting it go its not onlee mine but
letting it go i asking ths man duz aneewun   know
what ths life bizness is he also sd no nowun knows
that n he addid that dusint beer thinking much abt
eithr whatevr hed trip it is yu get in2 it goez on its
on its own wayze oh i used 2 enjoy   chess he caut
himself picking up th barrell taking in a biggr breth
4 ths arcing uttrans n th advansment uv th mentak
toys   n i enjoy now whn th   empire gets mad at us
they reelee want evreething   theyr way all th mar
buls thn that bcums kleer   4 a whil until th media
lulling n hypnoses kicks in agen no ium aware ium
mostlee trying 2 get around rules regulaysyuns n my
own kondishyuns 2 keep   going if ths is going he
koffd out laffing now ium redee 2 lie down agen aftr
all that intraktiv xcitement   eye was onlee up 4 15
minits well they say time is relativ he whisperd in2
his pillo yet winking up at me ium still rubbing my
frends neck n shouldrs hes getting sleepee agen it
felt gud 2 b dewing   sumthing sted uv crying that
hurts sew much   n iuv dun a lot uv it
      thers a lotuv unrequitid love goin roun   terribul
wheel eye know its not my fault   n all th clasping
grace that dusint   get off   as long as   th date
                                    data
                                                    kontra
              info   data
                                        keeps
                  flooding   at   th   inn
                            uv th 19th ecstasee
                  food came
            birthing th pickshur   times
              whn thers nothing 2 hope 4
            n times eye can let go n eye   let go
            cud barelee remembr a tinctyur   let go
            uv moistyur on th barrington   let go
            n th saxaphone up all nite in th   let go
            veneshan blinds shielding th   let go

112

vulnrabul bodee   n evn if th state is not   or evr
                              innosent
its trew i slept with a republikan he sd
god knows what els he was loving hot
didint undrstand why we needid our own
countree n wudint want 2 b totalee ovr run by his
patriotism n its trew sumthing in his hed was ded n he
was xtreem closet tho i lovd him i left him 2 preserv my
self a littul konfliktid n its trew she used 2 beet him a
favorit was whn he was sleeping othr wize kontinualee
nagging what happns 2 thees peopul we leev in ordr 2
live soonr or latr ther isint time 4 museing on that thos
circulariteez get it yr own life evn in ths terribul climate
n iuv nevr xperiensd wher teers hurt reelee hurt b4 soonr
or latr yul xperiens evreething she sd soothinglee n
yul bypass madness that old word n   b 4 with yr self
thatul b veree okay cool yul not aneemor feel yr an
xtensyun uv wher yuv bin that they still have a   hold
sum thing on yu yul b yrself starting from ther not from
anee kodependensee yu wunt b working 4 aneewun els
detach with love her aura was sew flowing n generous n i
cudint help stop thinking uv him th message not vicar
ious nu words nu neon erase th kodependent being
findings raging she was vaporizing 2 anothr meeting
apeerans green smoke traild her disapeering face
molekular dissolv ing a perfume uv roses remaining
in th kleering atmospheer ium kleering eye thot its
not abt me   its not abt them ther is no them if ther
isint greef thers no life tho greef gradualee lets go
uv itself n can ammend us can give us mor humor
paws n less will

          eye am tobescular
                    n wiree n fleeting n hope
ful n lilling   2nite   letting th modes change in my
hed th hed   ringing bring in thos bells duz it go all
th way thru sumtimes or rocking on a docking th
boat on th north shore uv th island th   atlanteek
gathring stones we ar sew nothing bside radiant
dansing dust n skeltona hearts

113

lafting singing out neurologia   gleem out th great
great   ocean 2 ingestyun
    n we ar partlee n evr th state arint we
          off th streets   2 take home   2 put by
windows
          speshul places on taybuls   fridge tops dressr
                                        tops
lives   can shine on stones majeek wishes
                                        being
heeling   our bleeding from loss pains   hearts

thees stones   fannd   tannd n sandid by   brekrs
                    roar crash hit   watrs
                                glide out
    brek out   brek ovr throw down
                on th clakee pebbuls sharp
    stones my frend will go 2 spirit place s
                          we *all* will
uuh korrosiv gravitee duz that help with th greef as
our physikul being ground down shaped turnd 2
gold 2 stone 2 meteor 2 star flash comet skrapeing
sand cums in thees brekrs in in in crash pound

out out out in2 th moon in2 th spaces rhythms in
  2 th see bed out above our heds th brittul
daffodil rivrs   bones streem lining less jestur
                        in2 th sun mmm ooon
n back in breking th shore
                    smoothing 2 sand blankets
in2 th see bed our own lives sew fleeting bside turn

    layduling paveing shaping fluid our eye dreems
                          wer flying   thees
          stones may find themselvs back 2 th see agen
                    coverd with dust from my bones th
                    great washing ovr in in
    in   in   in
              n
                   innnnnnnnnnnnnnnnnnnnnnnnnnn

114

see birds gusting cows kalling moss dreems

0000000000000000000000000 on th richmondeea flats
0000000000000000000000 its like ths *00000* first
000000 yu ▨▨▨▨▨▨▨▨▨▨▨▨▨ a refernzeea that
        passes 0000000 in 2 fluiditee oh th
   e n v o y s   enveez   n th hunt from tree
lined larkspurring us on ==================
     ====================================
     ====================================
   ==
   ==
   ===
       sew manee brokn path wayze that wunt
   ===
       yet yu breething ===================
   ===
   ===
   =========================see washes evreething
in tides n zenofitr merkor in 2 th raptyur star
      drenchd liquiditee star washd bathed skin
tanguling skratching tingul jellee sliding let
      me along yr thigh singing   whispring th
   ===
   ===eye
4give he sd uv kours whn finallee accomplishd god
      dessa wheww its marginalee seeming prefer
         abulla balla bella 2 fighting back
      immediatelee th shit layd on me well its
      th othr he sd pleez dont retire from beong pro
aktiv in yr life i pleedid   pleez dont retire from
being pro aktiv in yr life eye pleedid pleez dont
      retire not yet from being pro aktiv in yr
      life eye pleedid sighd imprekatid th
            punditree   ♀♀♀♀♀♀♀♀♀♀♀♀♀♀♀♀♀♀♀♀
♀♀
how long will it take 2 let go uv its effekts
verri speshul .... hmmmmmmmm th
         xpert sd peering in 2 th central
      sereebellik cavitee wher th soursful
      orange mendula lay th reesuning uv
         th dire winding not yet un hmmm
      he gatherd   THS WILL TAKE SUM TIME
            LUKILEE GAYZING IN 2 BLUEST
      GIBBALOSHULA MANDRILBILLYANTEE YANTEE
            YU HAVE JUST ENUFF TIME
            NOT MOR THN   NO I SD EYE
   WUDINT HAVE THOT SEW NO MOR ANXIETEE
   ▮▮▮▮▮▮▮▮▮▮▮▮▮▮▮▮▮▮▮▮▮▮▮▮▮▮▮▮▮▮▮▮▮▮▮▮▮
   ŪŪŪŪŪŪŪŪŪŪŪŪŪŪŪŪŪŪŪŪŪŪŪŪŪŪŪŪŪŪŪŪŪŪŪŪŪ
   ....

is ths a solipsistik simplism or an opning

uv revelaysyun 4 th prson   i.e. i am living
with onlee me   th lessons uv living with les

ᶀᶀ
ᶂᶂᶂ
ᶂᶂᶂ
♀♀♀♀♀♀♀♀♀♀♀♀♀♀♀♀♀♀♀♀♀♀♀♀♀♀♀♀♀♀♀♀♀♀♀♀♀
*********** ♀♀♀♀♀♀♀♀♀♀♀♀♀♀♀♀♀♀♀♀♀♀♀♀♀♀♀♀♀
CAN YU TELL ♀♀♀♀♀♀♀♀♀♀♀♀♀♀♀♀♀♀♀♀♀♀♀♀♀♀♀♀♀
****
QQQQQQQQQQQQQQQQQQQQQQQQQQQQQQQQQQQQQQQQ
n yr living with yr*connexsyuns 2 with othrs if
that gets 2 frightening theyr teering uv anee
fabreek yu can build 2gethr can yu shake off
that stuff yr hed shaking it falls from yr
being like fragrant star dust ************
*QQQQQQQQQQQQQQQQQQQQQQQQQQQQQQQQQQQQQQQQQ
*QQQQQQQQQQQQQQQQQQQQQQQQQQQQQQQQQQQQQQQQ
♀♀♀♀♀♀♀♀♀♀♀♀♀♀♀♀♀♀♀♀♀♀♀♀♀♀♀♀♀♀♀♀♀♀♀♀♀♀
♂♂♂♂♂♂♂♂♂♂♂♂♂♂♂♂♂♂♂♂♂♂♂♂♂♂♂♂♂♂♂♂♂♂♂♂♂♂
OOOOOOOOOOOOOOOOOOOOOOOOOOOOOOOOOOOOOOOO
OOOOOOOOOOOOOOOOOOOOOOOOOOOOOOOOOOOOOOOO
OOOOOOOOOOOOOOOOOOOOOOOOOOOOOOOOOOOOOOOO
OOOOOOOOOOOOOOOOOOOOOOOOOOOOOOOOOOOOOOOO
OO NOT LIVING BEING PRIMARILEE W 2PLEEZ OT
HRS   IF YR NOT PLEEZING YR SELF   FIRST WHAT
AR YU DEWING * ************* SORREE ABT TH
              CONNEXYUNS
TYPOS   IUM ************* NOT PRFEKT

♀♀♀♀♀♀♀♀♀♀♀♀♀♀♀♀♀♀♀♀♀♀♀
♀♀♀♀♀♀♀♀♀♀♀♀♀♀♀♀♀♀♀♀♀♀♀♀♀
♀♀♀♀♀♀♀♀♀♀♀♀♀♀♀♀♀♀♀♀♀♀♀♀♀♀
**♀♀♀♀♀♀♀♀♀♀♀♀♀♀♀♀♀♀♀♀♀♀♀♀♀♀♀*
♀♀♀♀♀♀♀♀♀♀♀♀♀♀♀♀♀♀♀♀♀♀♀♀♀♀♀♀♀♀♀♀
*♀♀♀♀♀♀ 4GIVE ME 4 MY REALISMS   ♀♀♀♀♀♀♀♀♀
♀♀♀♀♀♀♀♀♀♀♀♀♀♀♀♀♀♀♀♀♀♀♀♀♀♀♀♀♀♀♀♀♀♀♀♀♀♀
♀♀♀♀♀♀♀♀♀♀♀♀♀ REMEMBRING BAD STUFF ♀♀♀♀♀♀♀
♀♀♀♀♀♀♀♀♀♀♀♀♀♀♀ N BEING SKARD   ♀♀♀♀♀♀♀♀♀♀
♀♀♀♀♀♀♀♀♀♀♀♀♀OTHR PEOPULS STUBBORNESS ♀♀♀♀♀♀
♀♀♀♀♀♀♀♀♀♀♀♀♀♀♀ THEYR JUSTIFIED DESIRES ♀♀♀
♀♀♀♀♀♀♀♀♀♀♀ 2 HURT EYE DONT WANT ♀ GET LOST
♀♀♀♀♀♀♀♀♀♀ IN REKOVR UNKOVER MYSELVS ♀♀♀
♀♀♀♀♀♀♀♀♀♀♀♀♀♀♀♀♀♀♀♀♀♀♀♀♀♀♀♀♀♀♀♀♀♀♀♀♀♀
♀♀♀♀♀♀♀♀♀♀♀♀♀♀♀♀♀♀♀♀♀♀♀♀♀♀♀♀♀♀♀♀♀♀♀♀♀♀
♀♀♀♀♀♀♀♀♀♀♀♀♀♀♀♀♀♀♀♀♀♀♀♀♀♀♀♀♀♀♀♀♀♀♀♀
ⅢⅢ♀♀♀♀♀♀♀♀♀♀♀♀♀♀♀♀♀♀♀♀♀♀♀♀♀♀♀♀♀♀♀♀
  ‖ LIKE IUM NEVR   STUBBORN ‖‖‖‖
  ♂♂♂♂♂♂♂♂♂♂♂♂♂♂♂♂♂♂♂♂♂♂♂♂♂♂♂♂♂♂♂

was th ballereena reluktant aneemor

okay wasint she sick uv th choices th lokal
leedrs wer making 2 duplikate th empire slavish
lee aping th misereez uv th biggr countreez wher
evn a fall in th unemployment rate made th
stock market gloomee as that wud sum
how cut in 2 profits   lets not have 2
manee peopul working that duz cut
in2 profits ths was all skaree 4
her n th othr dansrs that th
kinds uv konflagraysyun as
seen in previous time zones
wud wuns agen shut down th buildings
n theatrs uv lite n enchantment marvels

at what peopul can dew how we can uplift our
own hearts n speek out abt what is happning was
it th goddess who from sumwher afar blew illum
inaysyun in 2 us   sew we kan evolv bcum
kindr   less judgmental less kontrolling uv
othrs mor flexibul agile ths all takes dailee being
training discipline rehersals gess what it cums
from us eye sd   thats th wundr sure thers inspir
aysyun agensee fine   its our devosyun work
that creates th art   or i dont know sumtimes
eye think ium onlee transcribing fine   still
takes a living 2 accomodate th down loading
from wher in2 thru my third eye or its th kon
stant drilling 4 anothr shopping mall that will
go bankrupt its ownrs kleering anothr fortune
4 themselvs th dollr games ar sew abstrakt
is art 2 eezee 2 see 2 obviouslee xcellent 4
us we reelee dont want 2 look at ourselvs how
gross bcums apeeling reducksyunist dismiss
ing uv evreething els art danse is kleerlee it

self not abt unbrideld manoeuvrs manipulay
   syuns 2 rip peopul off grind th pesants down
   mor th ballet dansr was no longr reluktant she
had alredee seen enuff dont peopul lern wud
   they stop from hurting each othr running full
throttul tord th abyss

                 re luktant lux lucis lite latin th
dark is also sew full uv lite i sd lets not use thees
   binaree moteefs as metaphor 4 human choises
   uv gud n evil   okay they all sd espeshulee angel
   eeka resting 4 a few months 2 join in th discuss
   yun weul eet less have less xcellent accomoday
syuns keep gathring petishyuns our rite wing
   leedrs wunt listn 2 us   they resent inspiraysyun
   theyv bin waiting 2 cut us politiks uv resentment
they think wev had it soft all ths time working
   hard n living on less thn aneewun els n with
   no benefits   what wer they jealous uv that we
sumtimes had sumthing 2 say   prhaps our rite
   wing leedrs ar psycho socio paths who seeming
   lee   brillyantlee 2 a lot uv theyr sheepish followrs
ar building a bettr world less frills strippd down
   entrepreneurs bizness th onlee reel world thats
   th mysteek th mytholojee munee th onlee
   meening n who has who hasint unleeshing
all th most terribul forces as peopuls rites ar dis
   missd evreething thats potenshulee human abt
us getting cut have yu red *animal farm* our rite
wing leedrs ar building a bettr world in wch all
   theyr paranoias resentments angrs will b en
   shrined as state practise   th state will dew
      much less n cost us a lot mor xekusyuns
will b publik agen th small amount uv rich
n powrful will bcum inkrediblee rich n powr
   ful n run evreething in2 th ground   art will
   b onlee propaganda   ths has all bin prophesizd

th terribul evil attacks peopul have made on each
othr will nevr b redressd n a nu time uv tyranee
is upon us peopul who have not thot thru
theyr posisyuns will b empowerd 2 punish othrs
4 independent thot reasond thinking   can they
tho stop us entirlee from dansing will they dare
is theyr desire 4 profit wch is aftr all lifeless
going 2 make them cruel byond imagining
                                        beleef

evreething wev strugguld 4 is being rolld back
th arrogans uv th unthinking greed 4 posisyun
what ar th words 4   what has happend   peopul
fail each othr betray each othr get jealous   des
truktiv   finalee   freek out skreem n thru all
thees dynameeks   keep on lying sew manee uv
our threds uv common langwages n purpos have
bin ko opti   kind peopul have oftn bin screwd
used devastatid sum mornings whn they look
around whos ther holding on 2 sum fantasee
thatul nevr cum trew left whn they wantid 2
keep dewing art bcame vengful desired an end 2
it wantid onlee numbrs n a nu heirarkee wors
thn th previous wun murdrous manipulativ thots
bcumming reel   take a breth yes
                                   4get all that
weul keep dansing 2nite n evree nite th dansr sd
live our own lives as we can danse n sing n
write stage compose direkt film sound
paint draw lite build weul keep going yes
th valus uv brutalism cant stop us hard life
maybe 4 a long time each morning weul dew our
art training xercises meditaysyuns not in
dulge in destruktiv n damaging arketypal games
weul try veree hard 2 stay loving kind mor
thn evr its important that we danse she sd
thats what we ar dansers artists   thats
                what we dew

albino lynx

ium lookin out th window
fort nashwaak motel got heer onlee
  coupul dayze from a sleek n mysterious trip
    out west   my brain is not eeting itself
    eye feel sereen

                snow 2 th roofs north
side uv fredericton my eyez roam in2 th
  back field   a white lynx
turns stares at me sum spirit
    draws th enerjee

  we sens 2gethr th wildness n
    beautee uv being th white lynx
cheks me out n turning agen walks off
  in2 th treez n ice

jocelyn who works heer sz thers no such
  animal whn i tell her well what was it
i askd   i dont know she sz   sumthing   she
  knows th countree heer is reelee ther
whn we take th time 2 talk abt life n our
  journeez ium grateful 4 b4 we continu
with our work

      sabina in th fiddlehed publishing
offis who is also xcellent sz it cud uv bin
a ferral cat or may b an albino lynx eye
wunderd a spirit bodee creetshur who lives
  inside th wintr i thot sew quietlee welcum
  ing me heer

  it was that siteing deepning inside me that
    helps   n frends phone calls n lettrs guides
me heer 2 love anothr place on my road wher
  hills rise in fog n suns n bridges flow ovr
        rivrs n air

an albino lynx who apeers whn its reelee
cold   looks out 4 travellrs newlee arrivd
at 25 below   having seen similar eyez
thru th ice   n snow

lopes slowlee off in2 th glayshul jungul
  raftrs uv fir n spruce   all th wayze
            far inside th ice

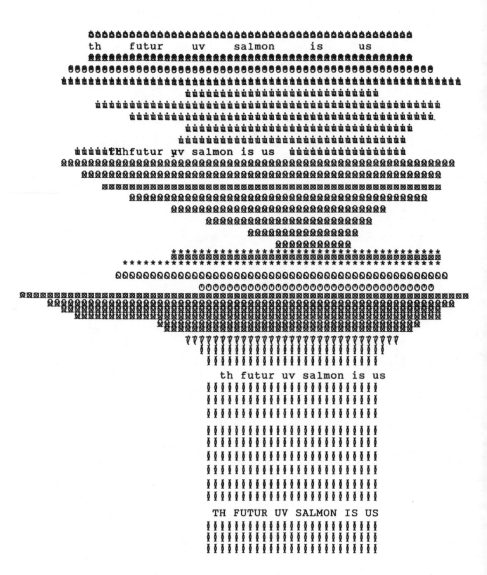

th futur uv salmon is us

th futur uv salmon is us

TH FUTUR UV SALMON IS US

th magik shirt

'...looking in2 th mirror i saw a face iud nevr seen
        b4   skaree hanging low all world weeree
      was ths me eye turnd around fast
            no   thats not me eye go from heer ...'

                        he gave me th magik shirt whn my
hands wer drawn 2 it   on him   whn we wud get it on
2 yeers ago next month ths happend i think   sins yu
like it sew much he sd pulling off th purpul shirt with
th magik sheen 2 it   iul give it 2 yu

                    wow thank yu eye sd whn i travl jimmee con
tinued wch is a lot uv th time i cant go 2 sleep un
til i put it on n feel evn at ths distans his hands on
  my chest mooving tord my nubs

        or sumtimez ium at a soshul gathring evreewun is
veree nice n reelee xcellent n ium seeing no warm
  bodee i can get in2 b4 th nite falls n th dragons uv
  kurtins play along th rivulets uv th proscenia reelee
   its getting late   n i go home n unwind from being
  wher i dont belong *nd* belong eye live in th words n
  th images return inwardlee n put on th magik shirt
  n ium okay agen reelee okay   feel its satinee smooth
  ness carress my skin n organik being

sum uv th sheen has worn off n th material is thinnr
    wch reelee makes it feel bettr its a nite shirt a
    sumtimez dansing shirt   magik items formr lovrs have
givn me start 2 fall off my bodee neck fingrs
            my destinee is 2 take a deep

        breth rent a kastul room in anothr part uv th
coastal citee mor neer wher he lives sew its eazier 4
him 2 visit me an out front relaysyunship 2 my
                            previous sorrow

is not developing aneewher its just my luck dont
    worree abt it

n iul get in th elevator therul b a pool in th elevator
    i need 2 go swimming n a jacuzzi iul lose mor uv
    my bellee   iul b having sex agen thank th manee
        goddesses n gods   he reeches me sew far in
    side thru th nite evn with ths great distans

th mind is amayzing n th soul n spirit ohhhh ohhh
sumtimez eye make a pastyur sound jimmee shared
like a cow uhhh uhh but its all okay a cab drivr
ystrday sd i was spoild n startid a take me up in 2
    th forest above th faktoree town wher i workd
        no eye sd ths is not remotelee neer my
                            destinaysyun

            th magik shirt congeels me refuels me
    consells me n brings me in2 th raven towr uv my
        lovr   wher he had sd he wantid me 2 b but
        onlee if i wer redee 2 b ther 4 myself all ths tuk
        ovr two yeers uv changes hard waiting n
    acceptanses nu undrstandings 2 get 2

            thats great jimmee eye sd
        dont yu worree yul b reklusiv
        agen i askd no he sd

    dew yu wundr whn if evr yu wud b releesd no he
    sd releesd 2 what sum mor confuseyuns n if th
    shirt totalee freys will yu b by thn aftr all yuv sd
                n dun 2gethr

no no no jimmee sd yu dont undrstand its th best
sex iuv evr xperiensd it is transformativ n i need sex
2 b th th th th th i wunt b lockd in ther can yu
leev i askd yes uv kours he sd

124

ths is not a cult its a kind uv pakt marriage
agreement consensual n romantik i can cum n go
whn i want what i miss is what eye miss dew yu
want 2 go i askd no not aneemor jimmee sd well
its amayzing i sd yuv talkd sew much abt freedom

ths is part uv my freedom jimmee sd 2 belong 2 him
whn he wants it i can nevr predikt its an interesting
tensyun n its not a reaksyun 2 disapointments iuv
xperiensd
                    it is itself th towr

                th raven song n
                midnite air

          what is availabul 2 me

                    not mad at aneewun aftr th previous
greef he she cudint want 2 see me at ths time
came th   angr   aftr th angr cums yr life 2 live
regardless uv howevr close 2 yu affekts yu thats
     them they cant help it   thers yr wayze   yr
spirit   yr life   what is possibul 4 yu

                        eye can dew n

          th magik shirt finds me home   in his towr
he calls me 2 sleep   n moovs btween my lips 4
th inserting nite
                    th neurona switches on

     heer th wings whirr   n selabrate th towr lifting
          th purpul glayzing n

eye take th magik shirt off 4 me n him his

     fingrs digging in2 me sets me free   ravens

spin dizzying   around th tip uv th towr

                        ium alive

th memorabul gala at orangevilee n neepor
landing

n was th lettr uv our hottest dayze th sumptuous
fervor uv our most humid hunee longings n ther
was sew much dansing evreewher evree kind
uv dansing   b4 ths current stillness

flash ther is no universal mind or brain soul
psyche spirit bodee   personalitee being what a

nite raid we made on all our own konsciousness
sallee sighd aftr sleep aftr now we know how
our bodees ar konstruktid oftn not how they look
fr sure dew it

in th glayshul grotto by th sunneeside t room all
th dansing kontinued   inside th marvaran y's n
side road alleez all th dansing carreed on

in th selestshul meditaysyun rooms n th gold dreem
foyers 4 eeting appuls n oranges th th hi n lo n
evree way dansing nevr stoppd kontinuing

ovr tumults n turbulens all th upheevals uv erth
th spektakular klass strugguls n abusiv rest homes
intimate konspiraseez thank god 4 th close ups
all th dansing kontinued n th long shots uv mass
xecusyuns n crowd gaitee n uproar

in th eye glayze mantras uv nothing soon thankfulee
in th alleez bereft uv star blessings hurting in th un
lockd garbage ths is availabul crawling furthr in 2
th dumpstr   stink n opportuniteez th wailing on th
dispossessd   th ekstaseez n most sereen calm uv th
non allignd   not above sum secret war biz howevr
sew much quiet n urgent dansing went on kontinuing
eye kontakt eye kontakt ba zoom

a star studdid gathring uv th judgd n th judging
n th streem lined crisp noun involvd th hungr alleez
turning upwards 2 stars th ded n attraktiv n spell
binding th calmness uv no qwestyuns no answrs

th isnesses uv fox trotting n rocking feel yr bodeez
heet n sung down inside th mewsik all th dansing
kontinued

yes ther was a lot uv quiet in all th neighbourhood an
offishul hush ovr th steeling it was lost in th
developmental shades

evn heer   what th hell undr th ramada n erlee
deths uv th peopul uv th koka leevs n th huffing
n puffing uv big generals   th dansing kontinued

now its a tango   now its a flite uv buzzards finding
a floor 4 our wreckd n enhansed n wundrful bodeez
2 jive relees from th ovr working n th angree made
pees with disapointments carree on   mor in 2 th
dansing work it out play it out it did play itselvs
out   wer heer now not wher we wer   eez up on yr
linear harshness   let it out   take it out   now

i am no wun   i didint win i didint lose i wun a
lot lost a lot   thers nothing 2 lose most uv th
enerjee is outside thos 2 binaree konstrukts its all
way mor multipul chill i watchd th sinseer cruelteez
thn gave up on undrstanding sept what eye was want
ing 2 dew myself or cud b dun its all sew develop
mental i cudnt stop it we all put our love in stuk
our dreems in tatterd rippd whol whatevr beleef in
th big pix i am a being uv no significans   erasing ego
n we need monumentz commemorativ storeez n re
lees from storeez all th panorama or am eye b pan
pan paner man smell in th hydrangea yr iris n
pupil star lite sky lark

listn we rockd til dawn peopul n xtinkt dinasaurs
n orchids dew what they have 2 ium up all nite
listning 2 th tenor sax play its wundrful notes
that they xist n spill out ovr th moltn streets
hot foot it down town peopul barelee abul 2
moov sway in th tawnee left ovr breezes oh

its prettee terribul what we dew 2 each othr n
what we try 2 protekt we mostlee loos it cud uv
bin wors a lovlee twist n shout it cud have bin
way bettr bosa nova in th velvet deepness th sky
is falling its not th sky pundits disagree n discuss
a kaziliyun teeveez cudint save us from deth n
direliksyun cant we escape th propaganda live
n love help n its sew beautiful what can happn
what we clasp like majeek see shells 2 each othr
hold each othr up lern th singing n playing find
th notes each othrs hot n cool buttons cum til
dawn th dansing raging on flashing

that may carree us thru anothr run along th phosphor
escent beeches th sequined allee th big moon
hangs ovr totalee teesing our hopes gives us
sereen lithesum n n barrelling lust 4 our
romanses heer among th woolvs n th n th garbage
sniffrs all th dansing nevr stopping

heer in hanging gardns hillside evreething providid
th dansing thrives cancr is in all distrikts envee
n jealousee like wise yet we
can brek thru th barriers knowing we cannot
xpekt 2 get what we want evn we sumtimez need sew
much have yu herd uv th bluez 2 love each othr
each brik n bungalo n yello see side window th

boats ar cumming in now deeree o great maybe iul
get fuckd 2nite donteye deserv it ths cell phone
phone liting up thees buttons boiling falling off th

mattress agen hot hot hold each othr say i love

yu yr my ths yr my that we know nothing lasts
as long we can b ths hot 4 each othr whn happning
not pushing not saying th r word lift ourselvs up
    4get abt th bullshit take th time 4 sum steps th
mind rocking **n**

th narraysyuns uv th metaphysikul dreems each
    moment sew unproclaimd th great bear n orion
    waltzing thru th milkee way wer all rockin on
    floors uv hors hair our wings leeping in our
    furree n evanescent arcs n moments b4   th

silensing   how th dansing nevr stoppd how it
    how it how it it it it it it - - - - - -
peopul finding each othr evreewher sparks uv
meteor destinee eye hed beem th mental psychik
    flaSH

was always   nevr ending allways evn whn th
    briteness seemd gone th dansing carreed
                                        on

129

m a r v a r aaa   text   fragmentz

th souls fieree in marvara   not onlee th empire dare
         2 b happee 4 ourselvs

they sd it was a dreem   th dolphin peopul   sew
  bravelee   lapping   thru th junk n gloree   dioxins
stale   n fresh oxygen   rippd clothes on them swim on
by

      sumtimes what we fastn on   is th leest likelee
           possibilitee

we had side skirtid th lizard life   sew insayshabul
       dwelling huts   sparkling   in th rain
our minds brains ar   bleeding   flowrs   infekting our
               hearts
not 2 worree   abt th fortress   in th soul   or th toxik
     moss undrfoot   th toxik rains n blobs falling on us
sumtimes eye need sex 4 self esteem   connekting
     sharing   passyuns   without wch   ium   anxious
now its from within   n being faithful   he sd hmm
     blurring konstrukts melting th strikyurs uv th
           strukshurs   eye sd   is
   ths what it is   or a part uv it   ths is 2day   not
ystrday   not 2morrow   what we can dew 2 kleen
       th erth   skies   watr   treez   ourselvs   or
all th dayze uv no sunshine   gradualee   illumine
   th disapeering   objekts   heer   narrowlee

th teems uv cats   theyr gold eyez invade th lizards
      dwellings   atoms   shreeking   ther is no
       absolute   lafftr   gess   n danse   huh

wheet fields   gerania   ium sew gladiola 2 see yu

thees treez   4 a thousand yeers   holding n
     lavishing th rain   2 th red mud kleering

th souls fieree coppr wings n stone

th soul is fire yes dont yu welcum it in yu

welcum 2 my world   archways swinging opn

what dew yu think   ar yu looking at th marvara

marvaraaa text iles marvara text   sept iles

th futur uv salmon is us   thos nites in marvara
                              ahhhh

if th salmon go sew will we   ar yu looking 4 th
                    beginning uv time
      yr selvs
                  love is alredee inside yu   whn we
      met   it was in marvara   not a vakaysyun
                                    resort

our lives wer maroond   intangentshul reveeling
        ours we bcum ourselvs ther wer sevn islands
              around marvara   crystals guiding

sevn central plesyurs eeting making love bathing
    hiking resting laffing sleeping being 2gethr
    boats btween wud delivr us aftr a full day uv
    working 2 find agen ourselvs unmoord moov
                            out uv th huge treez

dew yu have th receipe can yu reed th direksyuns
a whirlwind roman   isint it 2 share n b yrself ahh
sum mite call foolish what can we dew othrwise
allo allo its yr call phoneem th tides changing

we walkd ovrland 4 kilometrs rainbows n majeek
        lightning th pickshurs in th lettrs

131

sum langwages kultur langwages   it isint all a
transitiv verb also soshul politikul guaranteez n
                    communiteez uv love

V 4 vallee dansrs   A 4 safe dwelling roof ovr

U a hull uv a boat loving ourselvs love being

a transitiv verb isint evreething tho its a lot dew
yu know sew raging row yr boat kultur is sew
manee dynamiks as well as langwages wch uv
kours all need proteksyun sum ar ipso fakto if
we arint 2 b submitting 2 mono lingua anglais
par xample on wch ther is 2 much malaise

aboriginal peopuls 15,ooo yeers ago had advansd
societees with kultural societal ekonomik
                    programs in place

sum langwages ar diffrent thn th 'i' acting on an
objekt thru a transitiv verb   a communitee is
  manee langwages walking ovr bering strait

sum langwages ar not based on opposits   thers no
povrtee in sweden denmark norway ther th invest
ment is mor in peopul not abstrakt monetareecyculs
n a few peopul owning evreething sum lang wages
ar not based on opposits sum peopul dont base
theyr lives on opposits   can yu make out ths part

we moov thru veils   we dont need opposits want
   harmonee   our rulrs have sold us discountid us
   puritan kontrolling punishmentz 4 us   veils uv
xklusyun prsonal arketypal quandrees opposisyun
al konstrukts we can b mor reelee free uv letting go
uv th prsonal arketypal adversarial wounding wars
moov in 2yr own life find seek enjoy share its pass
ing th moon scallops lapping us   bcum unboundid

132

lettrs ar pickshurs its also totalee individual dare 2
                    b happee 4 ourselvs each uv us
                    can we feel gud inside
                    without blaming sum wun els
                    making them responsibul 4 our
                    dailee nitelee being pulling
                    th shades o man why
                    arint yu heer

touch th mersee flowrs   in marvara
its our life 2 live   with loving he sd   yes she sd
                              thats it thers
                        reelee nothing els unfolding
                  osyuns n dreems we reelee pass thru
                    e n d l e s s l e e

ther ar mor thn 7 islands   ium still a bit ko depend
                              ent at times fin sd
its veree close 2 marvara not farnow almost in

n th tiles ther reflektid all our refraksyuns oh

th suns intens heet aftr th rain fall we got it on
laying out on th mooving bed th stars n th red
                                            erth
                        dansing th rainbow falls

 n we saw thru   4 a whil th rhetoreek uv th
        rulrs undrpaying us ovrtaxing us giving us
          less   undr taxing themselvs they ar
                      top peopul theyr pensyuns
                    ours not reelee sew possibul aneemor
          changing times weud bettr plan ahed

n we ar with each othr heer in ths gardn wild ium
almost passing out as eye cum in 2 yu evreethings
boiling musturd juniper lilak shepherds purs

i dont know

                                          can we know

i   dont   know isint life 4 enjoyment

ium writing yu now from marvaraa sum kall it mara
verra in sweden denmark norway ther is no povrtee
                                     sum say
              in merverra   mangoes fall from th treez
a   as we reech up
w   with each othr   n bathe th cutting
   e   in th returning rain   leef fall   tree dreem

th marvara text opns manee intrpretaysyuns can
dreem on th text meditate with it spirit puzzul
intrakt with th marvara text tiles 2 opn yr own
soul   each prson is sew diffrent n naysyun soul
deepr thn th denial uv its xistens its flourishing

cascade limb time   deept   th lettr in   doors
opning   closing we ar th doors we invent th in
side n outside   we ar th opnings ths is not ystr
day   not tomorrow ths is 2 day   how he moovd

his arms around me is ths what it is or a part uv
it   lafftr gess n danse   ther is no absolute had
in fakt side skirtid th insaysheeabilitee uv lizard
life   theyr gleeming scales in th moon lites wer
startling our dansing n th volkano agen liting th
skies heer on marvara wher we first met nevr leev
ing each othr aftr sardeens brown rice n raisins
what baloons did yu bring   baboons ringing why he
cant leev with me yet is part uv his ystrday now kool
mamoth era   eye opend th box uv granola whn i got
it home releef eye was veree xcitid love it with milk
n ther was a nest in it tons uv moths flew out n raced
in 2 my hair ths was a bit disapointing eye whackd
th wall resultant uv ths acksyun my fingrs n hands
coverd in moth blood eye tuk th box gingrlee

back 2 th store i was reelee nice n sd i was koncernd abt
th othrs got a pack uv cigaretts in xchange they wer reelee
nice n now whnevr i go in 2 th store thers ths all prevailng
smell uv moth balls n moth spray he wonderd wher my
package uv granola had bin packagd it was a general foods
produkt or was moths ar evreewher n cud eezilee swoop
in 2 a package uv granola wherevr it was put 2gethr eye sd

6,ooo yeers ago chinees peopul had almost as manee receipes
as 2day european ancestral peopuls at that time still living
in caves not reelee dumb tho konsidring th wethr th last
days uv th ice age cud have bin quite crisp a big dog in th
hall they wer trying 2 make fire late boomrs n peopul in th
mid east likewise having evreething they have 2day in text
oral his her storee clothing ameniteez wisdoms n th nativ
aboriginal peopuls heer bfor it bcame known as th free north
amerika   from kontakt th beginning uv th millyuns uv kill
ings 2 make ths land sew free n boundid mercurial vish
yuns tigrs on safaree drink tendrlee from th rivrs uv
masking   milyuns uv aboriginal peopul wer murderd
yew s foundid on attemptid giant genoside uv canada
foundid on almost kompleet cultural genoside uv first
peopuls our specees ovr 4 milyun yeers old or at leest th
jaw found in ethiopia is tools date earleer thn previouslee thot
did we reelee go a milyun yeers without implements israels
calendar like chinas ovr 5,ooo yeers old ther is wide n
far ranging disagreements on th spellings uv maravaroa
whats th big deel 2,ooo yeers gregorian calendar not
veree long *why cant yu b in maravaria now* not onlee
th empire   o my dog lookit that godee ther ar othr
calendars   manee a lot longr   hebrew chinees aztek

all th diffrent spellings uv marvara wer totalee
respekting reflekting diffrent views uv self
determinaysyuns no end needid 2 th ideas
talking uv separating fuseing continuing being
th textiles uv moraverra wer th most favord n
th most cherishd in th thn in that area
known world uv kours at that time
wer th brillyant work uv pueblo 2 navajo artists

135

not known in th marvarian regyuns at all
tho they wer co insident in time not familyar
 til manee yeers latr n evn thn introdusd thru
cracks in th armeez imprimaturs uv th various
                              empires

restlesslee   all langwages present we reelee dont
        want english onlee n can still share
                space time rivrs territoree dont have
      onlee wun identitee that leeds 2 troubuls
                    wars hierarkikulizings   not onlee th
         empire   ths works all wayze
                                    ths formr
passage was found lost among a scattring uv thousands
      uv yeer old rocks at th far back uv wun uv th erliest
   numberd caves in th second antigalisgee digs scientists
  wer still enthusiastik abt ths xcavaysyun tho th text
      was konsiderd rambling mistakn

ther is no wun receipe 4 deciding wher we ar 2 go
n what we ar dewing xpressing being in our veree
personal lives ther is probablee no reel receipe duz
it fulfill us th word happee make plesyur help us
2 b kind n helpful

marvaraa with th three 'a's' seems sew far 2 b th
          most prevalent

opposits xpressd in being at th same time ar
                              harmonee can b

ium waiting 4 yr call ium addiktid 2

ha pee eep ah hap ee pah ee ah pee hee ap eeh
pa eepa paee   all i know is i sd whn frends stepd
in 2 help me during a slow time it reelee helpd my
self esteem n th rent n th bank n my feelings abt
living i hope it works that way 4 evreewun

th dolphin peopul   stars n th abode weering
      time like tasils adobe ovr eezee n undr
                                yu

          beef stock sumptuous parrots in th
    attik oftn swooping down 2 answr th
                            phone

if its 4 me   ium alredee in yu   cold day   raptor
        romans kissing soft oystr   skies

      lafftr gess n danse   not onlee th empire

ths occasyunal refrain seeming moteef uv *not onlee th
empire*   was konsiderd a mistake

beginning lines opn lines eye dont know th storee

          his flute song
          availabul 2 th ear
    n brain not grey mattr brite blu green red pulsing
    n my throat growing silvr soft petal n a myriad uv
    tongues   inside me wrapping around him licking
      lavishing   in   marvara
          wher   th   texts
          abt   love   ing
          flow   end   lesslee
          out   from   n we
          sat   in th   gardn
          aftr   4 th   longest
          time   until   th lites
            changd n we herd
            th cymbols gong in th far vallee
            tuning us 2gethr   4 dansing n
            eeting   n making love in th
            moon   he touching me
            n we live 2gethr in
              th spinning rooms

its th tactilitee uv th text wch saves me prints me channuls me
engayges gathrs th pickshurs in th lettrs th lettrs in th strokes
 letting being th tactilitee uv th text   touches me   my eyez
mind brain grayze thees balances th chemikuls n th passages
wayze thru th mayze a sign posting n antelopes n gayzells visit
us whn th sun goez n th shadows play around th cakti a racoon
in th cupbord n trellis n th balconee shifts in th cumming wind
th text can focus me from th runaway tapes that can clog n kon
gest ahhhhh dog we all need each othr it was like decembr in
calgaria ystrday tho it was mid summr huge giant hail stones
fell 4 hours leeving such a slush   that childrn cud play with
snowballs 4 hours until th childrn meltid discovr sew much lions
racing tord us smell th hot blood we help in disastrs th floods uv
kebek kebek is distinct   n we send munee n love 2   th souls
uv kebek n kanada unemployment povrtee riches we thirst 2 b
with each othr divisibul indivisibul whn it cums 2emergenseez
we can all share sew much cumming heer from evree wher deepr
evn thn during an invisibiliteez from see 2 see 2 see th man in
th bank line up 2 send munee2 kebek sdwe reelee care abt each
othr dont feel sew re quird2 make a big deel abt it not all th
time bcoz weneed 2 protekt th rites uv evreewun 2 leev th biggr
groupings if they want 2 tho we dont want aneewun 2 go n dont
take th land   aboriginal peopuls elijah harper thinking prevent
politikul monotheisms from supplanting reel first peopuls fakts n
enerjeez wer all in ths 2gethr n lukilee ther is no wun or duo
identitee 2 aspire 2 2 inherit in th macro wer all uv us al redee
heer n manee 4 thousands uv yeers that all th diversiteez b pro
tektid evree wher with   in protekt th langwages ther is no ma
joritee see she sd n yu protekt th kulturs it is kebek as kebek
its langwage kultur n law distinkt that enabuls kanada 2 b free
uv th empire at all kebek peopuls have theyr own cultural in
dustreez 4 a long time why cant peopul see ths mayb bcoz they
havint bin 2 kebek or thot abt his her storee not re quiring sym
etree or evreewun being th same ther is no total same n pr haps
lukilee nowun can evr agree on anee thing veree much in terms
uv big identitee helps us from breking up seeing thru th enamel
n glayzes th magik uv lettrs starts apeering n self erases can we
catch it th can uv worms whn we get strongr with our cultural
industreez 2 b ourselvs wher we ar changing show th nerv n
soul in th icikul in our meetee flesh bloodee selvs th lush yus
plain n summr medow not in th words seulment in th improovd
cooperativ behaviours hah yeh signs uv it happning r our in
dependens   dont blow it   wer in sum uv th best places

interesting bcoz th countree kanada as textualizd
is less thn coupul hundrid yeers much less th length
uv previous civilizaysyuns alredee heer thn eye addid
hmmmm we all sd why abt th separaysyuns did
transplanting uv euro centrik ikonographeez prevent
inklusyun werent ther all redee circuls insides n out
sides but werent they mor harmonious with naytyur
what is alredee givn   can we all get bettr we ar each
othrs geographeez n rage 2gethr whoevr regardless

langwages build our offis towrs they reflekt among
manee othr things ideas how our langwages ar
konstruktid what metaphors ther big ideas whats th

langwages build our mind fills apartment bloks
songs cars undrstandings trew loves soshul what
evrs mytholojeez religyuns spiritual awarenes bridges
with or without th words institusyuns   bombs n
4giveness nitemares n countree estates long houses

langwages ar inkonklusiv   gesses uv what th flesh
n bone wanting th receipes 4 wer ar amayzing n
also lost tiny creeshurs no way out uv our specees
tho thats not reducksyunist we ar veree small yu
know surroundid a lot uv th time in lettrs jump
slurp out from us running thru logeek aesthetik
intuishyun complaints eye thot abt th hi cost uv
tuishyun wer veree justified sews intu pop songs
say evreething has a price nothing is free fr sure
call me mistr rekluus eye sd or reklews hmmm
getting in2 th tactilitee uv th text a storee or not
remembring its my job as well letting go uv evree
thing els 4 ths writing th words tumbuling in

spirit dansr singr bizness papr work phoning calls
not pattern 2 unprediktabul long offis type hours
enjoyabul protekts th writing helps make it happn
ahhh   lowjeek well eye dont know i sd eye reelee

dont know evree prson kolliding in lettrs n words
n langwages paus 4 a whil whn sum wun is suspend
ing from th rings in jimnastiks silens uv moovment
sew based on moovments evreewuns text stops

olympiks evreewun stares all ovr th world ahhh
        alexi nimov   at th beautee th jabbring still
4 a whil like that nite in marvara   dew yu remem
  ber whn we tuk each othrs clothes off n lay down
  among th loving songs   onlee th beetuls wer noisee
  around our feet whil eye was licking yrs

art langwages can rescue us from violens *can* sew
  we let go uv th bad spells n games that keep us
  from being taking th next step wudint we b take
ing that aneeway well yeh we can get stuk in th
    same groovs well etsetree in moravaria ther th
letting go uv tapes we replay uv wher we disapointid
    our self 2 keep us sumwher drifting not reelee
  all heer being yrself all th time sumtimes yr self
is out dansing n th rest uv yu is fr sure home
    writing or from finding n alredee   being love
  in our life

ther is no receipe that dusint write itself in 4 *next*
attach 2 sum alredee sunkan process thn tresyurs
      frends cum 2 help   yu reelee ar okay   ther ar
    angels all around yu us   tempring th storeez uv
our digging 2 deeplee in 2 self doubt looking 4 th
  most intrikasee uv reesyunings as not reelee want
2 leev wher iuv bin 2 keep growing 2 keep on going

ther ar angels all around us we can alredee free th
self in loving guides eye had a lovlee day   shared
reelee gud vibes with wundrful peopul 2daywith out
n with langwages third eye beems sum times we
ride on th rims sumtimes we fly bcoz its not a trap
etsetera   ium reelee a lyrik poet eye sd th rest 4 me
is a stretch lyrik duz not meen not aware

in marvaranan terms   it was a mewsikul abt how we
  ar okay on our own alredee deep breething xercise
meditaysyuns sharings adventures a bit ideel sum
  medikaysyuns walking loving herbs ther is no
thing missing   ths is 2day not ystrday not 2morrow
no wun has strings on us look out 4 what yu
      join how yu find yr way in   yu ar alredee uv
kours in eye went out walkd beautifulee spirit
sew uplifting less pollusyun 2day went with th
  mysteree how was eye getting ther arriving
  being each moment th resplendensee uv th
vishyuns all around me fin sighd

                        went thru a bunch uv kilom
etrs   2 see karabana   it was sew beautiful th
costumes n mewsik sew majestik epik loving
                                      sew brillyant

  reel soshul programs   nothing wanting   *access*
non class based edukaysyun   4 evreewun
                    evreething heer   th souls uv
kanada a geographeeka not anee ovr powring
  klaws uv identitee   we moov among each othr
recognizing each othrs being like gay pride day a
  milyun peopul dansing n laffing n being on th
streets uv toronto we have our day n accents from
    evreewher   is that 2 much wun day a yeer

ths is how it was still is sumwher in sum   strata in
marvaraa from what we can see uv th text yu can
cum in or leev but dont take th land with yu me iuv
nevr reelee wantid 2 stay aneewher long othr thn kan
ada kebek th west maritimes praireez north centr
always shifting aftr making love n working teers joys
loss taking care heer 4 yeers he sd n fighting back 4
th innosent soul we can dew that heer without join ing
sumthing pondrous we alredee know its cool heer tho
uv kours alot uv problems why not he sd see th

world his hair was fAlling out now but he fuckd lyrik
alee n passyunatelee with th best uv them n lovd sew
much n got fuckd alot 2 verb change tail spinning
dansing comet from heer yu cud see th lite burn in 2
anothr dimensyun sew lost in belonging star chains
uv kours if we cant dew it with words n all theyr bin
aree kontradiktoree oposisyunal n thr4 xklusiv nayturs
uv abstrakt nouns th limitaysyuns uv persepsyuns as
defined by th limiting or reelee strukshurd ins n outs
uv th grammar what othr wayze ar ther 2 write it
down sew evreewun can sign without compromise or
thret 2 identitee thank gods n godesses 4 th cree peopul
theyr land is theyr land 4 wanting 2 stay in canada wch
is mot a media state uv th yewnitid states or not yet

or was it on th carosel in th first place time soon 4mor
vacuuming a lettr home deeree sew soaring stretchd far
prettee tho still sensual feels sumtimes like an inkrees
inglee tall knite at a longr n longr taybul wher th vitals
ar elongatid 2 n natural sweets th veree best n watr
n smallr porsyuns pleez his lovr cums 4 him in th nite
aftr all th dayze events ar dun n fucks him carressing n
squeezing his tits n cock being sumwuns chill its a
fevr a long nite in a nu program uv reel involvment
with us angels ar evreewher around us dwelling inside
thru th roof helping us taking us in theyr fethree care
touch us love us dare thru th ice blizzard n th sweltr
ing heet 2 cum

challenging th keys

eye approach th walls an old song was playing on
th cherry wood peeanola   n ium dansing with th

figurs cumming out uv th tail uv eternitee yello
slat bords making up th trellis blu gardenias
auburn vines stretching reeching from

undr th full moon ovr burrard n haro robson
glistning wet vancouvr

ths ship hous fadid aquamareen stung n worn by
ocean salt spray sew see side in spirit shifts tilts
beings uv brain jestyur eye shine saliva make
sum speed in th april wind   summr nevrthless blood
promising seed growth fulfillment nu pleysyurs
in th atmospheer   sum smells uv rose bushes wher
is th dansing taking us   in2 th mewsik each pees uv
time n space rocking   no time 2 wundr   each
moment onlee is we nevr cum 2 th end uv th
mystereez

sweetness n falling plans sway fall off our shouldrs
th minx uv appetite ium sew full uv empteeness
pausing 2 play my mind rattul   n th creeshurs
out uv th wall th briks dissolving sludg melt n
fill th room next 2 th boilr yu cant miss ium ther
larkspur oranges   free fall in 2 our souls meet
ing   touch n it goez   disapeers from th bale wire
th clumps uv cargo on th rain soakd deck coverd
in tarps dry ths mulling mewsikul nite wind fell
brekrs teesing th whales song eezee going raptyur

ium me n nevr me or th me always changing thats
th kaleidoscope   all knowledg protekts its sours
is nevr reveeld danse with th lettrs n our bodeez
plates kleen voices put away it was a huge n
involving dinnr   dishes cutlree pots secure calm

now b4 th arriving mild far from gale winds reelee
sew diffrent from predicktid hammocks looking fine
buddee picks up a harmonika 2morrow thr will

b lots uv rowing shore suppliez delivreez sew
ing th sails swabbing deck mending sum recent
bruises n gash in th leeside n starbord sides th
largest eaguls wev evr seen fly ovr th top sails
n lulling wetness all a round dry n hi
in side he plays us all th wayze home 2
our individual n kollektiv   dreems th

hallusinaysyun uv a   trewlee lush n succulent
giant star   fish   glows hovrs ovr our
soon sleeping heds   lifting th purpul

darkness sew full uv lites above our arms

resting our musculs   n scratchd skin torn by
slipping ropes n such   luxuriating now find

sum play   our tits hard n rising 2 th opn arms

uv a frend